MALDIVES TRAVEL GUIDE 2023-2024

The Ultimate Guide to Exploring the Indian Ocean's Best-Kept Secret

Bruce Terry

Copyrights © 2023 by Bruce Terry

All rights reserved. No part of this publication may be reproduced, distributed, or transmitted in any form or by any means, including photocopying, recording, or other electronic or mechanical methods, without the prior written permission of the publisher, except in the case of brief quotations embodied in critical reviews and certain other non-commercial uses permitted by copyright law

MAP OF MALDIVES

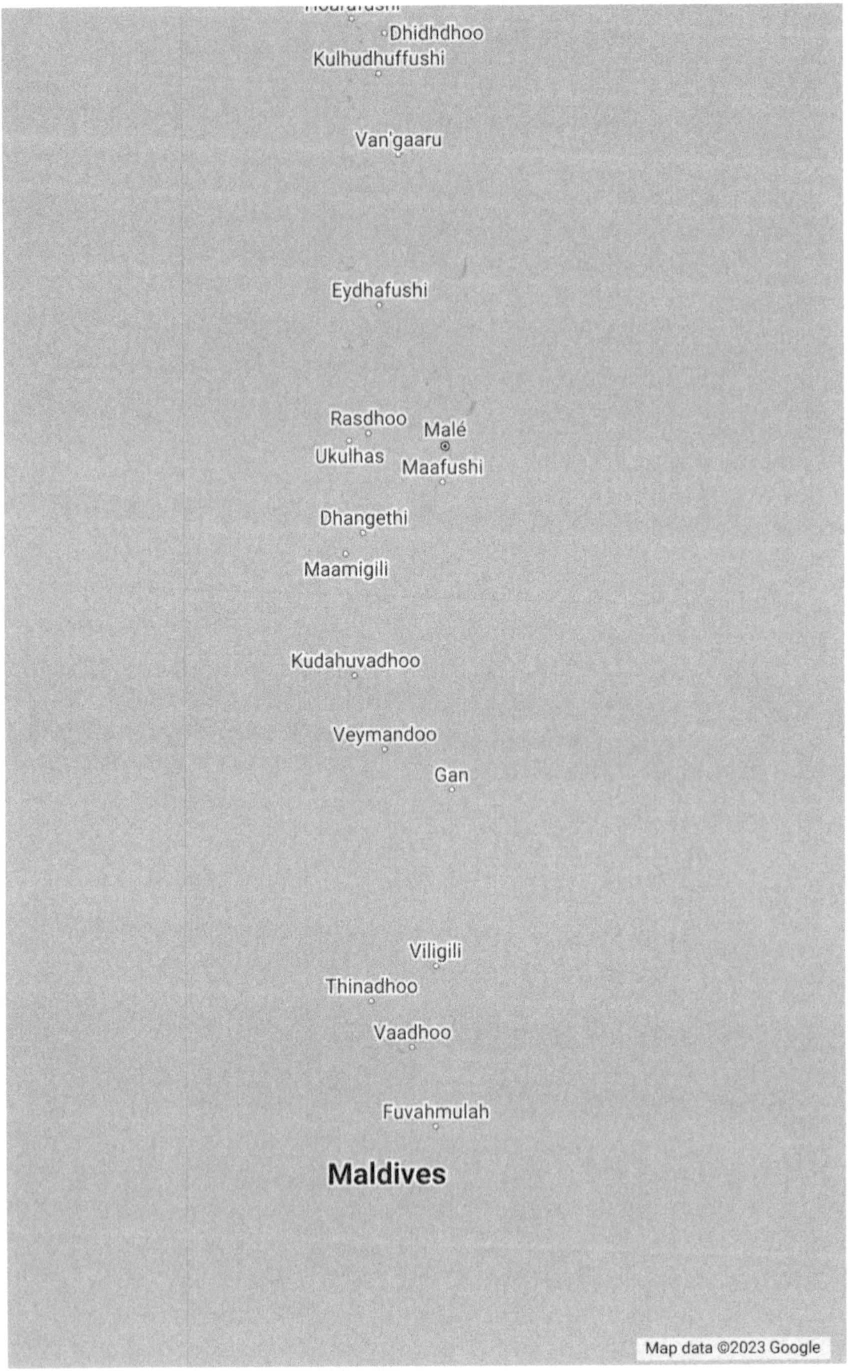
Dhidhdhoo
Kulhudhuffushi
Van'gaaru
Eydhafushi
Rasdhoo
Malé
Ukulhas
Maafushi
Dhangethi
Maamigili
Kudahuvadhoo
Veymandoo
Gan
Viligili
Thinadhoo
Vaadhoo
Fuvahmulah
Maldives
Map data ©2023 Google

TABLE OF CONTENTS

MAP OF MALDIVES 3

INTRODUCTION 9

    HISTORY 11

    GEOGRAPHY 14

    WEATHER 15

    CLIMATE 18

    10 REASONS WHY YOU SHOULD VISIT MALDIVES 20

CHAPTER 1 25

    GENERAL INFORMATION 25

- POPULATION 25
- PUBLIC HOLIDAY 27
- ELECTRIC PLUG 30
- CURRENCY 33
- LANGUAGE 35
- VISA REQUIREMENTS 38
- DIETARY RESTRICTIONS AND EATING 41
- TRAVEL INSURANCE 44
- CYBER CAFES 48

- TRAVEL PHRASES 52
- LOCAL TIME 55
- CREDIT CARD 58
- ATM 61

CHAPTER 2 65

BEST TIME TO VISIT MALDIVES 65

MONEY-SAVING TIPS WHEN VISITING MALDIVES 67

CHAPTER 3 73

GETTING AROUND MALDIVES 73

HOW TO GET FROM MALDIVES AIRPORT TO MALDIVES CITY CENTER 76

HOW TO GET FROM MALDIVES AIRPORT TO THE NEAREST HOTELS 79

PUBLIC WIFI AVAILABILITY IN MALDIVES 81

CHAPTER 4 85

WHAT YOU NEED TO PACK ON A TRIP TO MALDIVES 85

CHAPTER 5 89

TOP TOURIST DESTINATIONS IN MALDIVES 89

CHAPTER 6 95

BEST BEACHES IN MALDIVES 95

6 MALDIVES TRAVEL GUIDE 2023-2024

BEST RESTAURANTS IN MALDIVES 99

BUDGET-FRIENDLY HOTELS TO STAY 104

BEST LUXURY HOTELS TO STAY IN MALDIVES 109

BEST SHOPPING MALLS IN MALDIVES 114

BEST MUSEUMS IN MALDIVES 119

BEST PARKS AND GARDENS IN MALDIVES 124

BEST NIGHT CLUBS AND BARS IN MALDIVES 129

NIGHTLIFE IN MALDIVES 134

- ROMANTIC EVENING 134

FESTIVALS AND EVENTS IN MALDIVES 137

HEALTH AND SAFETY IN MALDIVES 140

PHARMACY AND FIRST AID 143

CHAPTER 7 147

FOOD AND DRINK 147

- LOCAL DRINKS 147

- STREET FOODS 151

CONCLUSION 157

8 MALDIVES TRAVEL GUIDE 2023-2024

INTRODUCTION

In the immense expanse of the Indian Ocean, a tropical paradise of incomparable beauty awaits. Welcome to the Maldives, a paradise famed for its beautiful beaches, crystal-clear blue seas, and colorful marine life. As the lovely ocean air caresses your skin and the golden light illuminates the horizon, you are about to start on an incredible adventure through one of the world's most beautiful archipelagos.

This travel guide is your key to revealing the mysteries of the Maldives in the year 2023-2024. Whether you are a passionate explorer, a hopeless romantic, or an inquisitive traveler, this paradise on earth offers an experience that exceeds imagination and leaves an unforgettable stamp on your spirit.

Beyond the lovely postcard pictures is a tapestry of colorful cultures, rich history, and magnificent natural treasures. Allow yourself to be involved in a universe where time slows down, and the problems of the outer world slip away.

From the busy capital city of Malé, where history and technology effortlessly combine, to the hidden islands that provide undisturbed peace, the Maldives has a treasure trove of surprises for every tourist.

Picture yourself swimming in the warm embrace of the water, entranced by the kaleidoscope of multicolored coral reefs and the beautiful dance of tropical fish. Imagine walking down powdered white beaches, your feet sinking into the soft sand as you soak in the beautiful warmth of the sun. Envision a night beneath a canopy of stars, the sound of the waves lulling you into a calm sleep in an overwater villa.

But the Maldives offers more than simply sun, beach, and sea. Delve further into its rich past, which includes stories of ancient mariners, magnificent sultanates, and the influences of diverse civilizations that have molded this island country.

Explore local marketplaces brimming with brilliant colors and perfumes, where you may sample the exquisite flavors of Maldivian food and connect with the warm-hearted inhabitants who exemplify the real spirit of island hospitality.

As you browse through the pages of this thorough travel book, you will unearth the hidden treasures of each atoll, discover the greatest diving places, and get suggestions for magnificent resorts that cater to your every whim. Whether you want adrenaline-pumping water sports, soul-soothing health retreats, or soul-stirring encounters with marine giants like whale sharks and manta rays, the Maldives provides a diversity of activities to suit every taste.

So, pack your luggage, set your compass towards paradise, and let this guide be your compass as you journey towards the Maldives in 2023-2024. Whether you are a first-time tourist or a seasoned traveler, this remarkable place will grab your heart, excite your senses, and leave you permanently under its spell. Get ready to make memories that will last a lifetime and go on a voyage through time and paradise.

HISTORY

The Maldives, formally known as the Republic of Maldives, is a tropical paradise situated in the Indian Ocean. Its history is rich and varied, extending back thousands of years. Let's discover the intriguing history of the Maldives from its first settlements to its present-day position as a prominent tourist destination.

Ancient Habitation and Early Kingdoms: The oldest evidence of human habitation in the Maldives goes back to roughly 1500 BCE. These early inhabitants were presumably Indo-Aryan migrants from the Indian subcontinent. The Maldives' strategic position along old trade routes led to its significance in the area.

By the 3rd century BCE, Buddhism had spread to the Maldives from India. The arrival of Buddhism had a tremendous impact on Maldivian society, culture, and language. The ancient Maldivian scripts, known as "Eveyla Akuru," were developed from the Brahmi script of ancient India.

Conversion to Islam and the Sultanate Era: The 12th century represented a key turning point in the history of the Maldives when Islam was brought to the islands. The conversion to Islam is reported to an Arab merchant and scholar, Abu al-Barakat Yusuf al-Barbari. Islam rapidly gained popularity and became the leading religion in the Maldives.

The embrace of Islam led to the formation of a centralized governmental structure. The Maldives went from a loosely structured collection of islands into a Sultanate. The oldest historical record of a Maldivian Sultan goes back to the 12th century.

Throughout the Sultanate period, the Maldives had strong relations with many regional powers, notably the Chola dynasty of South India and the Mughal Empire of North India. The islands also drew the interest of European colonial powers, such as the Portuguese and the Dutch, who desired to dominate the lucrative trade routes in the Indian Ocean.

Colonial Period and British Influence: In the 16th century, the Portuguese landed in the Maldives and imposed their influence over the islands. They formed a short-lived occupation, which lasted until the mid-17th century when the Maldivian monarch requested the aid of the Dutch to oust the Portuguese. The Dutch dominance, however, was short-lived, and by the late 18th century, the Maldives fell under the protection of the British Empire.

The British influence rapidly extended during the 19th century, and in 1887, the Maldives became a British protectorate. During this period, the Maldives had gains in infrastructure, education, and healthcare. However, the islands remained under British rule until 1965 when the Maldives won independence.

Freedom and Modern Development: After achieving freedom, the Maldives saw substantial political changes. The sultanate was dissolved in 1968, and the nation transitioned to a republic. Over the years, the Maldives endured political upheaval and periods of dictatorial government.

In recent decades, the Maldives has evolved as a popular tourist destination, recognized for its amazing natural beauty and clean beaches. The tourist sector has played a key part in the country's economic growth and development. The government has concentrated on sustainable tourism techniques to maintain the delicate nature of the islands.

However, the Maldives confronts issues such as climate change, as rising sea levels endanger the low-lying islands. The administration has been actively engaged in international climate change discussions, arguing for the protection of tiny island states.

GEOGRAPHY

The Maldives is a tropical paradise situated in the Indian Ocean, southwest of Sri Lanka. It is an archipelago consisting of 26 coral atolls, which are made up of more than 1,200 tiny islands. The nation runs over only 298 square kilometers, making it one of the smallest countries in the world in terms of both geographical size and population.

Atolls and Islands: The Maldives is noted for its unique geographical characteristic of atolls. Atolls are ring-shaped coral reefs that encircle a lagoon in the middle. The Maldives features 26 natural atolls, each consisting of several tiny coral islands.

These islands are sometimes referred to as "island resorts" and are popular tourist attractions. Out of the 26 atolls, some of the famous ones are North Male Atoll, Ari Atoll, Baa Atoll, and Haa Alif Atoll.

Island Formation: The islands in the Maldives are of coral origin. Coral reefs are generated by the aggregation of coral polyps, which secrete calcium carbonate to construct a strong exoskeleton. Over time, as the polyps expand and die, their exoskeletons pile, culminating in the construction of coral reefs. The islands in the Maldives are the tops of these underwater reefs, which have progressively risen above sea level.

Low-Lying Nature: One of the distinguishing features of the Maldives is its low-lying nature. The average height of the islands is just approximately 1.5 meters above sea level, with the highest point, Villingili Island, reaching a meager 2.4 meters. This makes the Maldives one of the flattest nations in the world. Due to its low height, the Maldives is very susceptible to the consequences of climate change, notably sea-level rise and storm surges.

Vegetation and Biodiversity: The Maldives enjoys a distinct and diversified marine ecology. The crystal-clear seas around the islands are home to beautiful coral reefs, seagrass beds, and a diverse diversity of aquatic life. The reefs sustain a multitude of marine wildlife, including colorful fish, turtles, rays, and even whale sharks. The Maldives is also recognized for its stunning white sandy beaches, which are typical of tropical islands.

WEATHER

The weather in the Maldives is affected by its geographical position, which provides it with a typical tropical climate typified by high temperatures, ample sunlight, and a distinct wet and dry season.

The Maldives has two primary seasons: the dry season (northeast monsoon) and the rainy season (southwest monsoon). These seasons are controlled by the monsoons, which are the prevalent wind patterns that bring shifts in weather patterns throughout the area.

The dry season in the Maldives extends from November to April and is characterized by clear skies, limited rainfall, and reduced humidity levels.

This month is considered the peak tourist season owing to the perfect weather conditions. The temperatures throughout this season vary from 25°C (77°F) to 31°C (88°F), giving guests warm and pleasant weather for outdoor activities, water sports, and sunbathing.

During the dry season, the Maldives sees generally calm winds, which makes it a wonderful time for diving and snorkeling aficionados to discover the brilliant coral reefs and rich marine life. The water clarity is high, and the sea is often calm, giving perfect conditions for underwater sports.

From May through October, the Maldives enters the rainy season, often known as the southwest monsoon. During this era, the weather is affected by damp breezes coming from the southwest. The rainy season is marked by higher humidity, a cloudier sky, and periodic rainfall. However, it's crucial to remember that the Maldives sees more sunlight even during the rainy season, with short rain showers frequently followed by clear skies.

The temperatures throughout the wet season remain warm, ranging from 26°C (79°F) to 31°C (88°F). The rainfall is more common, particularly in June, July, and August, with rare thunderstorms. However, rain showers are often short-lived and commonly occur during the late afternoon or evening, leaving most of the day bright and pleasant.

Despite the increasing rains, the rainy season still draws travelers who appreciate reduced accommodation prices and fewer people. Additionally, the Maldives' underwater visibility stays excellent even throughout this season, enabling travelers to discover the captivating marine life and enjoy numerous aquatic sports.

It's crucial to know that the Maldives' weather may be unexpected at times, and fluctuations within the seasons are conceivable. Weather patterns may vary swiftly, and short-term variations may occur. Therefore, it is essential to check the local weather forecast before arranging outside activities or trips.

In summary, the weather in the Maldives is tropical and defined by a dry season from November to April and a rainy season from May to October. The dry season delivers a bright sky, limited rainfall, and decreased humidity, offering perfect conditions for beach activities and water sports. The wet season provides somewhat higher humidity levels, intermittent showers, and cloudier sky, but still offers plenty of sunlight and possibilities for underwater exploration. Whether you travel during the dry or rainy season, the Maldives' natural beauty and pleasant temps make it a terrific vacation year-round.

CLIMATE

The climate of the Maldives is affected by its geographical position, with a mild tropical temperature prevailing throughout the year. Here, we shall investigate the climatic patterns, seasons, and weather conditions that define this gorgeous island country.

Tropical Monsoon Climate: The Maldives enjoys a tropical monsoon climate, which is defined by two distinct seasons - the dry season and the rainy season. The climate is affected by the monsoon winds, with the northeast monsoon (Iruvai) bringing the dry season and the southwest monsoon (Hulhangu) bringing the rainy season.

Dry Season (Iruvai): The dry season in the Maldives normally lasts from November to April, with December and January being the driest months. During this season, the northeast monsoon winds sweep through the area, resulting in generally calm and dry weather conditions.

The temperature during the dry season varies from 25°C (77°F) to 31°C (88°F), making it pleasantly warm.

The dry season is characterized by a clear sky, plentiful sunlight, and low humidity. This month is considered the peak tourist season since it provides great weather for beach activities, snorkeling, and diving. The crystal-clear waters, calm seas, and superb visibility make it an ideal time to explore the diverse marine life and coral reefs that the Maldives is famed for.

Wet Season (Hulhangu): The wet season in the Maldives extends from May through October, with peak rainfall being reported in June and July. During this season, the southwest monsoon winds bring moisture-laden clouds from the Indian Ocean, resulting in increased rainfall and occasional thunderstorms.

However, it's crucial to remember that even during the rainy season, rainfall is generally in the form of brief bursts or intermittent showers rather than continuous downpours.

The rainy season is marked by increased humidity and somewhat warmer temperatures, ranging from 27°C (81°F) to 32°C (90°F). Despite the increasing rains, the Maldives still enjoys a great amount of sunlight, and the sea temperature remains pleasant and appealing for swimming and aquatic sports.

Sea Level Increase and Climate Change: The Maldives, like many low-lying island states, is very susceptible to the consequences of climate change, notably sea level increase. Rising global temperatures lead to the melting of polar ice caps and thermal expansion of saltwater, culminating in the progressive increase of sea levels. This presents a huge danger to the Maldives since a substantial percentage of its landmass is just a few feet above sea level.

The Maldivian government has been actively engaged in climate change mitigation and adaptation initiatives, calling for global action to cut greenhouse gas emissions and developing steps to preserve the islands from sea level rise. Sustainable tourist practices, renewable energy efforts, and coral reef conservation projects are some of the actions done to maintain the Maldives' unique nature and economy.

10 REASONS WHY YOU SHOULD VISIT MALDIVES

Nestled in the center of the Indian Ocean, the Maldives is a tropical paradise that draws people from all over the globe. With its stunning white-sand beaches, crystal-clear turquoise seas, and opulent resorts, the Maldives provides a genuinely memorable experience.

In this essay, we will discuss the top 10 reasons why you should visit the Maldives.

Breathtaking Natural Beauty: The Maldives is recognized for its unrivaled natural beauty. Picture-perfect blue lagoons, vivid coral reefs, and lush tropical flora form a breathtaking setting for your holiday. Whether you're lazing on the beach or exploring the underwater world, the natural splendor of the Maldives is guaranteed to leave you in amazement.

World-Class Resorts and Accommodation: The Maldives is associated with luxury and provides some of the world's most exquisite resorts. From private villas suspended over the sea to magnificent beachside getaways, the Maldives has an incredible selection of housing alternatives that suit every need. Impeccable service, stunning vistas, and sumptuous facilities provide a wonderful stay.

Beautiful Beaches: With over 1,000 islands, the Maldives provides a plethora of beautiful, powder-soft beaches. These gorgeous lengths of sand beckon you to rest, unwind, and soak up the sun. Whether you're seeking tranquility or a vibrant scene, the Maldives offers a beach to fit your tastes, delivering an ideal beach vacation experience.

Incredible Snorkeling and Diving: The Maldives is a destination for snorkeling and diving aficionados. The crystal-clear seas are home to a diverse marine ecology teaming with colorful coral reefs, unusual fish, and even magnificent sea turtles and manta rays. With a wealth of dive sites catering to all levels of expertise, the Maldives provides an unequaled opportunity to explore the undersea world.

Water Sports and Adventure: Beyond snorkeling and diving, the Maldives provides a broad choice of water sports and adventure activities. From jet skiing and parasailing to windsurfing and kayaking, there is no lack of adrenaline-pumping thrills. The Maldives is the ideal playground for thrill-seekers and water sports lovers.

Romantic Getaway: If you're searching for a romantic location, the Maldives is the right option. With its isolated resorts, intimate dining choices, and magnificent sunsets, the Maldives sets the setting for an amazing romantic trip. Whether it's a honeymoon, anniversary celebration, or just a couple's vacation, the Maldives provides the ideal ambiance for romance.

Cultural Immersion: While the Maldives is famed for its natural beauty, it also boasts a rich and distinct culture ready to be experienced.

Visit the capital city of Male and see ancient sites, lively marketplaces, and vibrant local life. Engage with friendly people, sample real Maldivian food, and immerse yourself in the rich cultural history of the islands.

Spa & Wellness Retreats: The Maldives is a paradise for relaxation and regeneration. Many resorts include world-class spas providing a variety of therapies inspired by ancient healing practices. Pamper yourself with lavish spa services, yoga sessions, and wellness retreats in quiet settings, enabling you to completely relax and repair your mind, body, and spirit.

Unparalleled Sunsets and Stargazing: The Maldives delivers stunning sunsets that paint the sky in colors of orange, pink, and gold. As night descends, the absence of light pollution makes stargazing an incredible experience. The pure night sky displays a blanket of glittering stars, enabling you to marvel at the marvels of the cosmos.

Exclusivity and seclusion: One of the distinguishing aspects of the Maldives is its exclusivity and seclusion. With most resorts owning their islands, you may experience a feeling of isolation and tranquillity like no other.

Whether you're lazing by your pool or indulging in a romantic supper on the beach, the Maldives provides an exclusive and unique experience.

CHAPTER 1

GENERAL INFORMATION

- ## POPULATION

Population expansion: The population of Maldives has undergone tremendous expansion throughout the years. According to the World Bank, the expected population in 2021 was about 540,000. The growth rate has been substantially driven by factors such as lowering newborn mortality rates, better healthcare facilities, and a consistent rise in life expectancy.

Ethnic Composition: The Maldivian population is largely constituted of ethnic Maldivians, who make up almost 99% of the total population. Maldivians are an Indo-Aryan ethnic group with cultural and linguistic links to Sri Lanka and South India. The remainder population comprises expatriates, particularly from neighboring countries like India, Bangladesh, and Sri Lanka, who largely work in tourism, construction, and other areas.

Urbanization: The Maldives has witnessed substantial urbanization in recent decades, with a considerable concentration of the population in metropolitan areas.

The capital city of Malé, situated on the island of the same name, is the most heavily inhabited in the nation and serves as its economic and administrative core. Urbanization has been fueled by job opportunities, infrastructural development, and access to basic services.

Age Structure: The age structure of the Maldivian population exhibits fascinating trends. The bulk of the population falls into the working-age group (15-64 years), accounting for around 70% of the total population. This shows a reasonably youthful population with potential for economic output. The juvenile population (under 15 years) forms roughly 25% of the total, whereas the senior population (65 years and beyond) comprises a lesser fraction.

Population dispersal: The unusual terrain of the Maldives, consisting of 26 coral atolls and over 1,000 islands, offers difficulty to population dispersal. The bulk of the population is concentrated in the capital city and adjacent heavily inhabited islands. The remaining islands frequently have tiny populations, with some deserted or barely populated owing to their remote positions or inadequate resources.

Population issues: Despite the natural beauty and attraction of the Maldives, the nation has significant population issues. The tiny geographical area and limited resources put limits on sustainable development and the provision of basic services to the rising population. Additionally, the vulnerability of low-lying islands to climate change and increasing sea levels adds extra complexity to the demographic picture.

Conclusion: The population of Maldives shows a unique combination of indigenous Maldivians and a diversified expatriate community, with a rising population and a primarily youthful workforce. Urbanization and concentration of the population on important islands, together with demographic problems, are significant variables that define the country's demographics. Understanding the demographic dynamics of the Maldives is vital for policymakers and stakeholders to handle the possibilities and difficulties that emerge in supporting the well-being and development of the nation's residents.

- **PUBLIC HOLIDAY**

The Maldives also celebrates a multitude of official holidays throughout the year. These holidays give a unique opportunity to immerse oneself in the local culture, observe traditional festivals, and engage in real Maldivian experiences.

In this travel guide, we will cover the key public holidays of the Maldives, their importance, and how tourists may make the most of their vacation during these festive events.

Maldives Independence Day (26th July): Independence Day in Maldives marks the nation's independence from British colonial authority on 26th July 1965. The celebrations are distinguished by flag-raising ceremonies, parades, cultural performances, and spectacular street festivals. Travelers may see the patriotic passion by visiting the formal celebrations in the capital city of Malé, where the greatest rallies and processions take place. It's a wonderful chance to observe the national pride and learn about Maldivian history and traditions.

Republic Day (11th November): Republic Day in the Maldives marks the creation of the nation as a republic on 11th November 1968. The day is commemorated with considerable fervor, involving colorful parades, cultural events, traditional music, and dance displays. Travelers may connect with the local communities and enjoy the dynamic environment by attending the celebrations. Additionally, travelers may explore museums and historical places to dive deeper into the nation's journey to a republic.

Ramadan and Eid al-Fitr: Ramadan, the holy month of fasting celebrated by Muslims worldwide, carries enormous importance in the Maldives. The country's Muslim population observes fasting from dawn to sunset, engaged in prayers, introspection, and acts of charity.

While travelers are encouraged to observe the cultural customs and traditions during this month, they may still enjoy the unique environment in the Maldives during Ramadan. At nightfall, the neighboring towns come alive, with colorful street markets (known as "Hedhikaa") serving traditional Maldivian foods and cool beverages. The end of Ramadan is commemorated by Eid al-Fitr, a pleasant occasion when families assemble, special feasts are cooked, and presents are shared. Visitors may join locals in celebrating Eid, sharing meals, and enjoying the great hospitality of the Maldivian people.

National Day (1st January): National Day in the Maldives is observed on 1st January to commemorate the day the Maldives became a fully-fledged member of the United Nations in 1965. The day is honored by different cultural activities, performances, and fireworks displays.

Travelers may join in the celebrations, enjoying traditional music and dance displays, discovering local handicrafts, and relishing wonderful Maldivian food. This is also a fantastic chance to connect with people, learn their objectives, and obtain insights into the country's modern political scene.

Bodu Eid (Eid al-Adha): Bodu Eid, also known as Eid al-Adha or the Feast of Sacrifice is a prominent religious festival observed by Muslims worldwide. The Maldives celebrate this event with zeal when families assemble for prayers, exchange greetings, and indulge in feasts. The streets of Malé and other inhabited islands come alive with vivid decorations, and traditional Maldivian music fills the air. While visitors may not be allowed to join in the religious rites, they may still observe the celebratory attitude and appreciate the cultural diversity of the Maldives during this time.

- **ELECTRIC PLUG**

Traveling to the lovely tropical paradise of Maldives involves some preparation, and one key part is knowing the electric outlet system. Being informed of the sort of electric outlet used in the Maldives will guarantee that you can charge your gadgets and have a hassle-free vacation.

In this detailed guide, we will analyze the electric plug system in Maldives, give information on voltage and frequency, and provide some practical recommendations to bear in mind throughout your stay.

Electric Plug Types: The typical electric plug used in the Maldives is Type G, popularly known as the British three-pin plug. It includes three rectangular pins, with the top pin being somewhat longer and thicker than the other two. This style of plug is extensively used in the United Kingdom, Ireland, and numerous other countries, making it reasonably simple to acquire appropriate converters or chargers.

Voltage and Frequency: In Maldives, the electrical voltage used is 230 volts, which is comparable to several European nations.

Therefore, if your equipment is intended for a different voltage, you may require a voltage converter or a device with a built-in voltage converter to prevent hurting your electronics. Additionally, the frequency in Maldives is 50 Hz, therefore confirm that your gadgets are compatible with this frequency.

Adapters and Converters: To guarantee that your electronics can be connected to the Maldivian power outlets, you will need a compatible adaptor. As indicated previously, Type G plugs are used in the Maldives, thus purchasing a Type G adaptor before your travel is necessary. Adapters may be obtained online or at most travel accessory retailers. It is preferable to purchase a global adapter that can be used in other countries, enabling you to use it beyond your Maldives vacation.

If your equipment is not compatible with 230 volts, you will additionally need a voltage converter. A voltage converter can change the voltage from 230 volts to the needed voltage for your equipment. Be careful to verify the power rating of your gadgets and buy a converter that can handle the appropriate watts.

Power Outlets in Accommodations: Most accommodations in the Maldives, including hotels and resorts, feature power outlets compatible with Type G plugs. However, it is usually a good idea to clarify this with your accommodation ahead. Some higher-end resorts may have universal outlets that accommodate several plug types, avoiding the need for an adaptor.

Practical Tips:

Here are some practical suggestions to bear in mind about electric outlets in the Maldives:

a. It is preferable to bring a multi-plug power strip or a USB charging hub to charge many devices concurrently. This will spare you from the headache of looking for several adapters or converters.

b. It is advisable to include your adapters and converters in your carry-on baggage so that you have access to them immediately upon arrival in the Maldives.

c. If you forget to bring an adaptor or converter, certain resorts, and hotels may give them for hire or loan. However, availability cannot be assured, therefore it is always preferable to arrive prepared.

d. Ensure that your electrical gadgets are compatible with the voltage and frequency in the Maldives. Check the specs or labels on your gadgets or follow the manufacturer's instructions to prevent any harm.

Conclusion: Understanding the electric plug system in Maldives is vital for a smooth and pleasant stay. By understanding the plug type, voltage, and frequency, and by being prepared with the proper adapters or converters, you can simply charge your equipment and enjoy your stay in this tropical paradise without any electrical problems. Remember to prepare ahead, bring the right adapters, and always emphasize safety while dealing with power during your vacation to the Maldives.

- **CURRENCY**

When planning a vacation to the gorgeous archipelago of the Maldives, it is vital to educate yourself about the money used in the nation. The national currency of Maldives is the Maldivian Rufiyaa (MVR), and knowing its denominations, conversion rates, and availability can assist guarantee a seamless financial experience throughout your stay. In this travel guide, we will present a full explanation of the currency of Maldives to assist you manage monetary concerns with confidence.

Maldivian Rufiyaa (MVR): The Maldivian Rufiyaa is the national currency of the Maldives. It was created in 1981, replacing the Maldivian Rupee. The currency is governed by the Maldives Monetary Authority (MMA), which controls the issue and circulation of banknotes and coins.

Banknotes and Coins: The Maldivian Rufiyaa is available in both banknotes and coins. Banknotes are issued in denominations of 5, 10, 20, 50, 100, and 500 Rufiyaa. These banknotes have brilliant colors, elaborate patterns, and local themes, making them visually attractive. Coins, on the other hand, are available in denominations of 1 and 2 Rufiyaa, as well as 1, 2, 5, 10, 25, and 50 Laari (1 Rufiyaa = 100 Laari).

Conversion Rates: It is vital to be informed of the conversion rates while changing your local money to Maldivian Rufiyaa. Exchange rates might vary depending on the supplier, such as banks, authorized exchange agencies, or hotels. It is recommended to check rates and fees to guarantee you receive the greatest bargain. Additionally, be aware that prices may vary owing to worldwide currency exchange markets, so it's a good idea to check for any big currency swings before your trip.

Currency Exchange: Currency exchange services are commonly accessible in Maldives, notably in attractive tourist regions and major airports. Banks and authorized exchange bureaus are the most dependable sources for exchanging currencies. It is advisable to exchange your money at these official institutions rather than via street sellers to prevent counterfeit notes or unjust prices. ATMs are also popular in populous locations and may be utilized for money withdrawal, mainly in Maldivian Rufiyaa.

Tipping Culture: Tipping is not generally practiced in the Maldives since a service fee is typically included in the bill. However, if you experience great treatment or desire to express thanks, a little tip is accepted but not required. It is recommended to provide gratuities in Maldivian Rufiyaa or the local cash equivalent.

Currency limits and Import/Export Regulations: There are no limits on the import or export of the Maldivian Rufiyaa. However, if you are carrying an amount above USD 10,000 (or equivalent), you must disclose it at arrival or departure.

- **LANGUAGE**

It's necessary to acquaint oneself with the official language of the nation. As a prominent tourist destination renowned for its magnificent beaches, stunning resorts, and rich marine life, Maldives provides an unforgettable experience to travelers from across the globe. In this travel guide, we will study the official language of Maldives, Dhivehi, and give you essential information to improve your vacation experience.

Dhivehi: The National Language: The Maldivian people, commonly known as Maldivians, mostly speak Dhivehi, which is the official and national language of Maldives. Dhivehi is an Indo-Aryan language, closely linked to Sinhalese and Divehi, and bears some characteristics with the languages spoken in Sri Lanka and southern India.

While Dhivehi is largely spoken in Maldives, it is also used by Maldivian populations living in adjacent countries.

Language Characteristics: Dhivehi is written in the Thaana script, a unique writing system composed of 24 letters. This script is derived from Arabic and is read from right to left. The Thaana script provides for the depiction of all the sounds in the Dhivehi language, making it an effective and complete writing system.

The pronunciation of Dhivehi may be problematic for non-native speakers owing to its peculiar phonetic qualities. The language has its unique set of sounds that may not exist in other languages. However, English is commonly spoken in tourist regions, resorts, and among younger people, making communication reasonably simple for travelers.

Language and Cultural Etiquette:

When visiting a foreign country, learning the local culture and etiquette is crucial to guarantee a courteous and pleasurable trip. In Maldives, it is acceptable to welcome someone with a smile and a brief "Assalaamu alaikum" (hello) when entering a room or meeting someone. It is also usual to remove your shoes before entering a local's house or a mosque.

Respecting the local customs and traditions is vital, and a basic comprehension of Dhivehi words will help you demonstrate your appreciation for the local culture. While many Maldivians are competent in English, making an effort to learn a few Dhivehi words would be welcomed by the locals and may establish a deeper connection during your stay.

Language Resources: To further strengthen your grasp of Dhivehi, you may explore many language resources accessible online, including language learning applications, phrasebooks, and online language courses. These tools may help you establish a basic comprehension of the language and enhance your communication abilities throughout your trip.

Additionally, local Maldivian residents, resort workers, or tour guides may frequently give useful insights into the language and culture. Don't hesitate to engage in talks with them to learn more about Dhivehi and the rich history of the Maldives.

Conclusion: As you begin on your adventure to Maldives, adopting the national language, Dhivehi, may enrich your travel experience by creating ties with the local people and immersing yourself in the dynamic culture. While English is commonly spoken, making an effort to acquire a few simple Dhivehi words may go a long way in demonstrating respect and admiration for the Maldivian culture. Immerse yourself in the splendor

- **VISA REQUIREMENTS**

To guarantee a simple and hassle-free vacation, it's crucial to acquaint yourself with the visa requirements before making travel plans to this tropical paradise. We will give you a thorough overview of the visa requirements for visiting the Maldives in this article.

Visa-Free Entry: Citizens of several nations are eligible for visa-free travel to the Maldives. You don't need a visa to visit the Maldives and may remain there for a certain amount of time if you have a valid passport from one of the following countries:

Entry without a visa for 30 days:

Australia, Canada, New Zealand, the United States, Japan, South Korea, Malaysia, Singapore, and Thailand are all members of the European Union (EU).

90-day visa-free entry for citizens of Brazil and South Africa:

Uruguay, Chile, and Argentina

Visa on Arrival: The Maldives provides a Visa on Arrival (VoA) option for visitors from nations that are not included in the category of those who do not need a visa to enter. As a result, travelers may get a visa at the Maldives' international airports. The

VoA is normally granted for 30 days, although it may be extended for a maximum of 90 days.

The following conditions must be met for you to be eligible for a VoA:

A passport having an expiry date of at least six months.

A ticket for a guaranteed departure or return.

Evidence of your lodging throughout your visit.

Sufficient money (at least $100 a day) to meet your costs.

It's vital to remember that Maldivian immigration officials have the option to award VoAs. Although it is often a simple process, it is advised to have all the required paperwork on hand to speed up the arrival formalities.

Pre-Arrival Visa: You may apply for a pre-arrival visa via the Maldives' diplomatic missions overseas if you are not qualified for visa-free admission or would like to have your visa prepared before going. The pre-arrival visa, sometimes referred to as a tourist visa, may be renewed for up to 90 days and is only valid for a maximum of 30 days.

To apply for a pre-arrival visa, you must provide the following paperwork:

A finished visa application.

A passport with a minimum six-month expiration date.

Two current passport-size images.

Flight itineraries provide evidence of travel reservations.

Evidence of lodging (a letter of invitation from a host or a hotel reservation).

Sufficient money to meet your stay's expenditures.

To give yourself enough processing time, it is advised to apply for the pre-arrival visa well in advance of your intended trip dates.

Visa Extensions: You may request a visa extension via the Maldives Immigration office if you want to prolong your stay over the original visa validity. Up to a total stay of 90 days, extensions are allowed in increments of 30 days.

You must provide the following paperwork to get a visa extension:

A completed application for a visa extension.

A passport that is valid for at least six months.

Proof that you have the money to pay for your prolonged stay.

An official return or onward ticket.

Evidence of accommodations for the extra time.

To prevent any legal issues, you should start the extension procedure at least a week before your existing visa expires.

Conclusion: To guarantee a smooth and pleasurable holiday, it is essential to comprehend the visa requirements for visiting the Maldives. Whether you are entitled to access without a visa, prefer the ease of a Visa on Arrival, or choose to get a pre-arrival visa, be sure to comply with the appropriate papers and adhere to the rules established by the Maldivian authorities. Before your journey, don't forget to review the most recent criteria and updates to remain informed of any changes to the visa regulations. You may go on a fantastic visit to the lovely islands of the Maldives if you make the necessary preparations.

- **DIETARY RESTRICTIONS AND EATING**

For a good dining experience, it is crucial to be aware of the dietary limitations and eating alternatives accessible.

This travel guide will provide you with a thorough overview of dietary requirements and dining in the Maldives, including insightful information on local cuisine, eating habits, and meeting different dietary demands.

Local Cuisine: Fresh fish and tropical ingredients are emphasized in Maldivian cuisine, which is a combination of Indian, Sri Lankan, and Arabic tastes. Fish is the primary source of food in the Maldives, and several meals are made using tuna, reef fish, and other kinds of seafood. Popular Maldivian foods include Rihaakuru (thick fish paste), Mas Huni (mashed tuna with spices and coconut), and Garudhiya (fish soup).

Dietary Restrictions:

Halal Food: The Maldives is an Islamic country, and the vast majority of its citizens adhere to Islamic dietary restrictions. Since halal cuisine is widely accessible across the nation, Muslim guests may choose from a variety of dishes without any hesitation.

Despite Maldivian cuisine's traditional focus on seafood, vegetarians and vegans traveling there should not be concerned. The majority of hotels and eateries include vegetarian and vegan menus with meals created with seasonal, locally-sourced fruits, vegetables, lentils, and spices. There are additional possibilities for eating foreign food that are suitable for vegans.

Gluten-free needs and allergies: Many businesses in the Maldives are acquainted with these conditions. Resorts and eateries are often flexible and may adjust meals or provide substitutes to satisfy certain dietary restrictions. To guarantee a pleasant eating experience, it is advised to let the restaurant know in advance about any dietary limitations you may have.

Food alternatives: If you are staying at a resort in the Maldives, you will have a choice of food alternatives at your disposal. Numerous restaurants providing a variety of cuisines, including Maldivian, Asian, Mediterranean, and more, are often available at resorts. It is typical to have buffets and à la carte menus, which let you choose items that, suit your dietary requirements.

Local cafés and restaurants: You may find local eateries that serve both residents and visitors in crowded locations like Malé, the nation's capital. These restaurants provide a blend of Maldivian and foreign food, allowing visitors to experience real tastes and interacts with locals.

Despite its scarcity, Maldivian street food provides a distinctive gastronomic experience. Small food carts often provide traditional treats like "hedhikaa" for sale. It's crucial to remember that the street food scene may not offer many alternatives for those with certain dietary needs, so use care and let the sellers know what you need.

The Maldives provides safe drinking water in resorts and urban areas, although it is advised to drink bottled water to prevent any possible health problems.

Food Safety: To reduce the risk of contracting a foodborne illness, it is advised to consume cooked food, and peelable fruits, and steer clear of raw or undercooked seafood.

Communication: Be sure to let the staff or chef know about any dietary restrictions or food allergies when making meal reservations. This will guarantee that they can cook proper meals and any necessary adjustments if necessary.

In conclusion, a crucial component of your trip experience should be discovering the gastronomic wonders of the Maldives. You may enjoy the tastes of this gorgeous location while maintaining your unique dietary requirements by being acquainted with the regional cuisine, being aware of dietary limitations, and looking for suitable eating alternatives. Remember to explain your needs in advance, be willing to try new foods, and enjoy the Maldives' diverse cultural offerings.

- **TRAVEL INSURANCE**

Consider travel insurance when you plan your trip to the Maldives to safeguard yourself against unanticipated events that might interfere with your holiday. We will examine the significance of travel insurance for the Maldives in this extensive guide and highlight important aspects to take into account when choosing coverage.

Why Maldives is travel insurance necessary?

A crucial component of every vacation, including one to the Maldives, is travel insurance. For your trip to the Maldives, travel insurance is essential for the following reasons:

Emergency medical care, including hospitalization, emergency medical evacuation, and repatriation, are all covered by travel insurance. The Maldives is a far-off location, and some of the islands may not have many medical services. If you have travel insurance, you may acquire the required medical care without having to pay a significant price.

Vacation Cancellation or Interruption: Since life is unpredictable, there may be instances when you must cancel or shorten your vacation due to unanticipated events like sickness, accident, or a family emergency. You may be entitled to reimbursement for non-refundable costs such as airfare, lodging, and activities if you have travel insurance.

Lost or Delayed Baggage: Travel plans might be ruined by lost or delayed baggage. Travel insurance ensures you have the necessities while waiting for your stuff by covering the cost of replacing important goods and offering reimbursement for luggage delays.

Travel Delays: Weather conditions or other unforeseen circumstances may result in flight cancellations or delays. In such circumstances, travel insurance may provide extra coverage for costs like lodging, food, and transportation.

Emergency Evacuation: The Maldives is an archipelago of islands, and travel insurance may help with the expenses of emergency evacuations in the case of a natural catastrophe or civil upheaval.

What qualities need to travel insurance coverage?

Take into account the following elements while choosing travel insurance for your trip to the Maldives:

Medical Protection Examine: the insurance to make sure that it offers sufficient coverage for medical costs, emergency medical evacuation, and repatriation. It must address any present medical issues as well as any planned activities, such as scuba diving.

Trip Cancellation/Interruption: Seek a policy that reimburses non-refundable charges if a trip is canceled or interrupted for one of the listed reasons, such as sickness, injury, or unforeseeable circumstances.

Baggage and Personal Belongings: Confirm the reimbursement for necessary things if the luggage is delayed, as well as the coverage for lost, stolen, or damaged baggage.

Travel Delay Coverage: **Verify the insurance pays for extra costs incurred as a result of travel delays, such as lodging, food, and other transportation.**

Check whether the insurance company has emergency support services that are available around the clock, including a hotline you may call in case of emergencies or if you need travel guidance.

Additional factors to think about include

Activities Coverage: **Verify that your travel insurance coverage covers adventurous activities like snorkeling, diving, or water sports. For high-risk activities, several insurers provide an optional coverage option.**

Policy Exclusions: **To understand what is not covered, carefully read the policy exclusions. Pre-existing medical issues, risky conduct, or involvement in illicit activities are examples of frequent exclusions.**

Policy restrictions: **Pay close attention to policy restrictions, such as the maximum coverage sums for luggage, trip cancellation, and medical expenditures. Make sure they match your trip requirements and probable costs.**

If your journey lasts longer than the initial coverage term, check the policy's length and if it may be extended or renewed while you are away from home.

Where can you purchase travel protection?

Travel agencies, trustworthy insurance companies, and websites that specialize in travel insurance are all good places to get travel insurance. Before choosing a policy, compare them all, read client testimonials, and take customer service, pricing, and coverage into account.

An essential element of any vacation to the Maldives is travel insurance. It offers financial security and peace of mind while protecting you from unforeseen catastrophes. Find a comprehensive coverage that prioritizes covering your unique requirements, such as unexpected medical expenses, trip cancellation/interruption, lost luggage, and travel delays. You can relax and enjoy your Maldives holiday knowing that you have the correct travel insurance, giving you a safety net in paradise.

- **CYBER CAFES**

Cyber cafés are a hidden treasure for tech-savvy visitors. These cyber cafés serve individuals who still need to remain connected, catch up on work, or just enjoy some online amusement, even though the majority of travelers to the Maldives are looking for a digital detox. We'll examine the Maldives' internet café sector in more detail in this travel guide, going through their characteristics, locations, and the services they provide.

Infrastructure and connectivity: The Maldives has a stable telecommunications network that offers nationwide internet service. Excellent broadband coverage is available in the main cities and important tourist locations, making it simple for travelers to access the internet. The cyber cafés in the Maldives make full use of this infrastructure by providing their clients with high-speed internet connection.

Cyber café features include:

State-of-the-art Equipment: To provide a pleasant and effective surfing experience, cyber cafés in the Maldives are furnished with cutting-edge computers, high-resolution displays, and ergonomic seats. To assure peak performance, the equipment is routinely serviced.

Private Workstations: To increase privacy and lessen distractions, most cybercafés provide private workstations with partitions or dividers. Professionals who need a peaceful area to concentrate on their job may find this feature to be very useful.

Gaming Zones: Many cybercafés in the Maldives designate sections for gamers in addition to workstations. These areas provide a variety of popular games and strong gaming PCs equipped with the newest technology.

Snacks and drinks: To improve the experience, cyber cafés often offer a small café or snack bar where patrons may get a quick snack or a drink while using the internet.

Locations of Cyber Cafés:

There are several places where you may find a cyber café in the Maldives, including:

Malé: The capital and largest city of the Maldives, Malé, offers several internet cafés that are conveniently positioned across the city's many districts. They are conveniently located near major hotels, retail malls, and tourist destinations, making them accessible to visitors on foot.

Tourist Resorts: The Maldives is home to several opulent resorts that value connection and provide their visitors access to internet cafés. These resorts provide guests with a tranquil setting and breathtaking views, enabling them to work or surf the internet in solitude.

Major Islands: Major tourist islands including Maafushi, Hulhumale, and Guraidhoo also have cyber cafés. These islands are perfect locations to discover cyber cafés since they provide a lively environment and a variety of activities for tourists.

Services Provided

Cyber cafés in the Maldives provide a high-speed internet connection with a range of data packages to accommodate diverse demands and price ranges. Most cafés charge fair prices, and some even offer hourly or daily packages.

Printing and scanning services: are often available in cyber cafés, which is helpful for tourists who need to print tickets, documentation, or other important papers.

Online gaming: Gamers may interact with others online or participate in multiplayer games while playing a variety of games at cybercafés.

Technical Support: Cyber cafés often have knowledgeable staff members who may provide technical support if any problems with the tools or internet access occur.

While the Maldives are known for their stunning natural scenery and peaceful environment, internet cafés provide visitors with a unique way to remain connected and take care of their digital demands. The cyber cafés in the Maldives provide dependable internet connection, up-to-date technology, and a pleasant setting, whether you need to catch up on work, chat with loved ones, or engage in online gaming. So, the next time you're in this tropical haven, be sure to stop by a cybercafé and take advantage of the best of both worlds.

- **TRAVEL PHRASES**

While English is widely spoken in tourist areas, learning a few basic travel phrases in the local language, Dhivehi, can enhance your travel experience and show respect for the local culture. In this travel guide, we will provide you with a list of essential travel phrases to help you navigate the Maldives and connect with the locals.

Greetings and Basic Expressions:

Hello: Assalaamu alaikum (pronounced: ah-sah-lah-moo ah-lah-koom)

Goodbye: Dhannavan (pronounced: dha-na-van)

Thank you: Shukuriyaa (pronounced: shoo-koo-ree-ya)

Please: Adhes kohfa (pronounced: ah-des koh-fah)

Excuse me: Ma-aaf kohfa kurey (pronounced: mah-ahf koh-fah koo-ray)

Yes: Aan (pronounced: ahn)

No: Noon (pronounced: noo-n)

Asking for Directions:

Where is...?: ... kihaa gahdhuneh? (pronounced: ... kee-ha gah-dhoo-neh)

How do I get to...?: ... eygeh kaley kihaa hen'dhuneh? (pronounced: ... ay-geh ka-ley kee-ha hen-dhoo-neh)

Left: Hulhugali (pronounced: hool-hoo-gah-lee)

Right: Edugali (pronounced: ay-doo-gah-lee)

Straight ahead: Geygandeh (pronounced: gay-gan-deh)

Basic Phrases for Shopping and Dining:

How much does it cost?: Kihaa badhah dhanee? (pronounced: kee-ha bah-dah dah-nee)

I would like...: Aharengey... (pronounced: ah-ha-ren-geh)

Water: Uru (pronounced: oo-roo)

Food: Hedhun (pronounced: heh-dhoo-n)

Delicious: Fahun (pronounced: fa-hoon)

Emergency Phrases:

Help: Adhuvas (pronounced: ah-dhoo-vas)

I need a doctor: Aharengey dawas kameh vaane? (pronounced: ah-ha-ren-geh dah-was ka-meh vah-neh)

Where is the hospital?: Hosheedhungey kihaa gahdhuneh? (pronounced: ho-shee-dhoo-geh kee-ha gah-dhoo-neh)

Call the police: Dhaandhen vanee (pronounced: dhaan-dhen vah-neh)

Social Etiquette:

What is your name?: Kon nameh kiyanee? (pronounced: kon nah-meh kee-yah-neh)

My name is...: Aharengey nameh... (pronounced: ah-ha-ren-geh nah-meh)

Nice to meet you: Balaadhugandeh dhanee (pronounced: bah-lah-dhoo-gan-deh dah-nee)

Sorry: Ma-aaf kohfa (pronounced: mah-ahf koh-fah)

Can you help me, please?: Aharengey dheynuneh, adhes kohfa kurey? (pronounced: ah-ha-ren-geh dey-noo-neh, ah-des koh-fah koo-ray)

Conclusion:

By familiarizing yourself with these essential travel phrases in Dhivehi, you'll have the opportunity to engage with locals, enhance your cultural experience, and navigate the beautiful islands of the Maldives more comfortably. Remember, even attempting a few basic phrases can go a long way in showing respect and creating connections with the local people. Enjoy your trip to the Maldives and immerse yourself in its captivating beauty and warm hospitality!

- **LOCAL TIME**

To get the most out of your visit, it's crucial to take the local time into account while making travel plans to this lovely archipelago. We will go into detail on the local time in the Maldives in this travel guide, including its time zone, daylight saving time, and advice for preventing jet lag.

The Maldives adhere to Maldives Time (MVT), which is UTC+5, all year round. It is important to note that since the Maldives do not follow daylight saving time, the time is constant all year long.

The time zone is shared with several other nations in the area, including Sri Lanka. It is essential to modify your plans and timetables by the local time in the Maldives while making your vacation itinerary.

Coordinated Universal Time (UTC): Using Coordinated Universal Time (UTC), it is easier to comprehend local time in the Maldives. Because Maldives Time is five hours ahead of UTC, if it is noon in the United States, it will be 5:00 in the Maldives. In contrast, if it is 5:00 AM in the Maldives, it will be midnight UTC. You can efficiently plan your flights, lodging, and activities by keeping this time zone in mind.

Jet Lag Management: To lessen the effects of jet lag, tourists arriving in the Maldives from other time zones may need to acclimate to the local time. Here are some suggestions for preventing jet lag:

Gradual Adjustment: In the days leading up to your vacation, gradually change the times you go to bed and get up depending on which way you want to travel. Your body may be able to adjust to the new time zone more quickly as a result.

Drink lots of water before, during, and after your flight to stay hydrated. Keeping hydrated might assist with jet lag symptoms including weariness and headaches.

Exposure to Natural Light: Daily exposure to natural light is important once you arrive in the Maldives. This assists in regulating the biological clock in your body and assisting with time zone adjustment.

Avoid Napping: Try to fight the urge to take a long snooze when you first arrive. Instead, take part in leisurely activities and go to bed at a decent hour. This will help with a quicker transition to the new time zone.

Melatonin pills: which may assist regulate your sleep habits and make the change to the local time easier, should be discussed with a healthcare provider.

You may lessen the effects of jet lag and make the most of your stay in the Maldives by using the tactics listed below.

A seamless and pleasurable journey to the Maldives requires that you be aware of the local time. Maldives Time (MVT), which is UTC+5, is observed year-round in the Maldives. To get the most out of your trip, it's a good idea to plan your flights, activities, and lodging around the local time.

 Additionally, you may adjust to the new time zone more successfully by treating jet lag with gradual adjustment, water, exposure to natural light, avoiding lengthy naps, and using melatonin supplements. Therefore, take a seat back, relax, and take in the beauty of the Maldives knowing that you are on local time.

- **CREDIT CARD**

It's crucial to comprehend the accessible payment alternatives to make your journey to this tropical paradise as easy as possible. In the Maldives, credit cards are widely accepted and provide ease, security, and several other advantages. The specifics of using credit cards in the Maldives will be covered in full in this travel guide, including accepted card networks, acceptance rates, considerations for the local currency, and advice for a hassle-free trip.

Popular Credit Card Networks: Visa, Mastercard, and American Express are the most commonly used credit card networks in the Maldives. The majority of hotels, resorts, restaurants, stores, and tourist sites around the nation accept credit cards thanks to these networks.

Credit cards are frequently accepted in the Maldives, particularly at well-known tourist destinations, upmarket resorts, and bigger institutions. It's important to keep in mind that smaller companies, neighborhood shops, and lodging establishments can prefer cash payments.

The native currency, Maldivian Rufiyaa (MVR), is thus advised to have on hand just in case. However, credit cards continue to be the go-to payment option for bigger purchases in the majority of tourist regions.

The official currency of the Maldives is the Maldivian Rufiyaa (MVR), however, US dollars (USD) are also commonly accepted everywhere in the nation. You may choose between paying with your credit card in MVR or USD. It's crucial to remember that paying in USD can result in extra charges or a less advantageous exchange rate. Therefore, to avoid any possible additional fees, it is often advised to pay in the local currency.

When using your credit card to make a transaction in the Maldives, you can come across a service called Dynamic Currency Conversion (DCC). Instead of using the local currency, DCC enables you to make payments in your currency. Although it can appear handy, this often entails higher exchange rates and extra costs. It's advised to deny DCC and choose to pay in the local currency to guarantee you obtain the lowest rates.

Contactless Payments: Also referred to as "tap-and-go," contactless payments have grown in popularity around the globe, and the Maldives is no exception. Numerous businesses, especially those serving foreign visitors, accept contactless payments.

Most credit cards include this capability, which enables you to do rapid and secure transactions without having to insert your card or enter a PIN.

Benefits and Security: There are various benefits to using a credit card in the Maldives. First off, carrying huge amounts of cash is no longer necessary, lowering the possibility of theft or loss. Credit cards also come with built-in fraud protection and dispute resolution processes that safeguard your finances. Numerous credit cards also have rewards programs, such as cashback or travel miles, which may be very helpful for regular travelers.

Precautions and advice:

Let your credit card company know: Before leaving for the Maldives, let your credit card company know that you'll be there. This keeps them from surmising fraud when they see transactions coming from another nation.

Carry several cards: It's a good idea to carry at least two different credit cards from separate networks so you have a fallback in case one of your cards is lost, stolen, or not accepted elsewhere.

Confirm if there are any extra costs for overseas transactions with your credit card: To save expenses, look for credit cards that have no or minimal international transaction fees.

Despite the widespread use of credit cards, keeping some emergency cash in local currency is crucial, particularly for small businesses or unforeseen circumstances where cards could not be accepted.

While it is possible to withdraw money from ATMs in the Maldives, use caution to avoid potential skimming devices or fraudulent operations. Reputable locations with ATMs, including banks or hotels, should always be used.

In conclusion, credit cards are a practical and common form of payment in the Maldives. They benefit passengers in addition to offering security and convenience. You may have a hassle-free experience making payments during your trip to this alluring tropical location by being aware of the widely used credit card networks, taking currency conversions into account, and taking a few safety measures.

- ATM

It is crucial to be well-prepared before traveling to the tropical paradise of the Maldives, particularly when it comes to handling your funds. A pleasant and easy experience during your stay in the Maldives will be guaranteed if you are aware of the location and operation of ATMs.

We will examine all facets of ATMs in the Maldives, including their locations, acceptable currencies, fees, and practical advice for using them efficiently, in this thorough travel guide.

ATM Locations: There are many ATMs in the Maldives, especially in well-liked tourist areas like the capital city of Malé and the main resort islands. ATMs are available in many places, including airports, retail centers, banks, and resorts. Before your arrival, it is a good idea to locate the closest ATM to your lodging, ensuring that you always have quick access to cash.

Accepted Currencies: The Maldivian Rufiyaa (MVR) is the country of the Maldives' official currency. It is crucial to remember that the majority of Maldivian ATMs also give out US dollars (USD) in addition to local money. This is because resorts, hotels, and other tourist destinations around the nation often take US currency. To cover various expenditures, it is advised to carry both USD and MVR.

Transaction costs: It's crucial to be aware of any possible transaction costs while using ATMs in the Maldives. For cash withdrawals, foreign cards often charge a fee. Depending on your bank and the kind of card you are using, the fees may change. It is essential to speak with your bank in advance of your travel to learn more about the precise charges that could be imposed.

It is advisable to enquire in advance about these costs since certain ATMs in resorts could additionally impose extra convenience fees.

There are usually daily withdrawal limitations at ATMs in the Maldives. Depending on the ATM and the card you are using, these restrictions may change.

To find out your daily withdrawal cap, it is best to call your bank in advance. It may be advantageous to let your bank know ahead of time that you will want more cash and ask for a temporary increase in your withdrawal limit.

Advice for Using ATMs:

Let your bank know: Inform your bank of your vacation before going to the Maldives to prevent any possible problems with your card being stopped because of suspicious behavior. Giving them information about your trip's dates and location can assist to guarantee continuous access to your money.

Carry numerous cards as a backup in case one is lost: stolen, or rejected by an ATM. It is advised to carry extra debit or credit cards. You will benefit from an extra level of convenience and security as a result.

Pay attention to your surroundings: Use care and be mindful of your surroundings while using an ATM. Select sites that are safe and well-lit, especially inside banks or other respectable businesses. Before exiting the ATM, make sure to retrieve your card and the transaction receipt, conceal your PIN input from inquisitive eyes, and collect your card.

Despite the accessibility of ATMs, it's always a good idea to have some emergency cash on hand in case of unforeseen circumstances. Both local money (MVR) and US dollars (USD), which may be quickly converted if necessary, may be used.

Conclusion: A hassle-free and delightful trip may be made possible by being aware of the nuances of utilizing ATMs in the Maldives. You may comfortably handle your funds and have access to cash whenever required by being acquainted with the places, currencies, costs, and helpful advice included in this travel guide. Being organized and ensuring easy financial transactions will help you make the most of your vacation in this beautiful archipelago.

CHAPTER 2

BEST TIME TO VISIT MALDIVES

The ideal time to visit the Maldives will be discussed in this guide, taking into consideration the weather, seasonal changes, and particular activities that are accessible at certain times of the year.

Peak Season (November to April): The dry northeast monsoon falls during the Maldives' peak season (November to April), providing tourists with the perfect weather for an unforgettable trip. The weather at this time is characterized by a clear sky, low humidity, and little precipitation.

77°F to 86°F is the range of typical temperatures, which creates a comfortable tropical environment. It is ideal for snorkeling, diving, and other water sports because of the calm waters and superb underwater visibility. It's crucial to keep in mind that this is also the busiest time of year for tourists, which means that lodging costs will go up and there will be more people on famous islands.

The dry northeast monsoon gives way to the moist southwest monsoon during the shoulder seasons (May and October). These months are regarded as the shoulder seasons, and although having a little bit more rainfall than the high season, they still provide a good time to visit the Maldives. With temperatures between 25°C and 31°C (77°F and 88°F), the climate is still warm. The shoulder seasons are a great option for frugal tourists who want to escape the crowds since they strike a mix between cost and pleasant weather.

Low Season (June to September): The rainy season, also known as the southwest monsoon, falls during the low season in the Maldives. The islands endure increased humidity and more frequent, often brief, rain during this time.

It's crucial to remember that the Maldives have a tropical climate, which means there are often bright days and clear skies even during the rainy season. Between 75°F and 86°F, the average temperature is between 24°C and 30°C. The low season has several benefits, including fewer visitors, cheaper lodging, and the chance to see marine species like manta rays and whale sharks, even if the weather may be less dependable.

Particular Points to Consider

Surfing: If you like the sport, peak surfing season, which lasts from May to October, is the finest time to visit the Maldives. The islands enjoy more waves at this time, drawing surfers from all around the globe.

Diving: The Maldives are well known for their excellent diving options. While diving is possible all year long, the greatest visibility and circumstances are often found from November to April, which is peak season.

Manta Rays and Whale Sharks: If swimming with manta rays and whale sharks is your top priority, you might think about traveling during the low season, which runs from June to September.

The ideal time to go to the Maldives will mainly rely on your tastes, financial situation, and itinerary. Although the peak season has the best weather, it also has the highest pricing and most visitors.

The weather is most pleasant and prices are most reasonable during the shoulder seasons. In contrast, the low season offers a special chance to explore the Maldives at a slower pace and see fascinating marine species. You may plan your trip to the Maldives for an amazing holiday in paradise by taking these aspects and your particular tastes into account.

MONEY-SAVING TIPS WHEN VISITING MALDIVES

The Maldives might be pricey, but there are several ways to save costs without sacrificing a special trip. This post will provide you with 20 suggestions for saving money when traveling to the Maldives, enabling you to get the most out of your vacation without going over budget.

Travel during the off-peak season: Going to the Maldives when it's less crowded might help you save money. In comparison to the high season, hotels and airlines often offer reduced prices and discounts from May to November.

Spend some time researching and comparing rates for flights lodging and activities: before making your travel arrangements. For the greatest offers and savings, use online travel agents and hotel booking websites.

Choose guesthouses or nearby islands: Instead of booking a stay at a five-star resort, give guesthouses or nearby islands a thought. These choices provide a chance to explore local culture and engage with the Maldivian community and are often cheaper.

Create an island-hopping itinerary: Think about island-hopping rather than spending the whole time at one resort. You may encounter many places and broaden your experiences without spending more money by traveling to several islands.

Book all-inclusive packages: When making a resort reservation, think about going all-inclusive. These packages often come with meals, beverages, and activities, giving you more for your money than if you were to pay for everything individually.

Utilize public transportation: Getting to the Maldives is inexpensive with local ferries and public transit. To avoid paying for inter-island transit, research the ferry times and adjust your route.

Eat at neighborhood restaurants and cafes: Local eateries will provide you with a taste of real Maldivian food at more reasonable costs, while resort dining might be pricey. Try traditional foods like fish curry and mas huni as you explore the local culinary scene.

Carry a reusable water bottle; the cost of buying bottled water over time may mount up. Bring a reusable water bottle instead, and fill it up at your hotel or guesthouse, or other places with clean water. This simple action may decrease plastic waste and help save money.

In the Maldives, snorkeling is a preferred pastime: Bring your equipment. Bring your snorkeling gear to avoid paying rental costs rather than renting at each place.

Examine activities that are free or inexpensive: The Maldives has a number of them. Take strolls on the beach, go snorkeling at the house reef, or just relax and take in the natural beauty all around you without having to pay any further money.

While resorts provide a variety of activities: such as water sports and excursions, they may sometimes be rather pricey. To prevent overpaying, set priorities and choose the activities that most appeal to you.

Booking activities directly with local providers: If you do decide to partake in certain activities or excursions, think about doing so. When compared to resorts or travel companies, they often offer lower costs.

Negotiate pricing at local markets: Don't be scared to haggle while purchasing souvenirs or regional crafts. In the Maldives, haggling is a typical activity, and you may be able to get a better bargain.

Limit your alcohol intake: since it is usually pricey in the Maldives owing to hefty taxes. You may want to minimize your alcohol intake or get duty-free drinks at the airport before you arrive.

Use the free facilities offered by the resort: If you decide to stay there, make use of the free services they provide. To save money on entertainment, make use of the resort's pool, fitness center, and free activities.

Avoid things that are not necessary: Be aware of additional costs and levies that may add up rapidly. Refuse superfluous services, don't use the minibar in your hotel, and carefully verify your statement before you pay to guarantee accuracy.

Look for group or package discounts: If you're on a group trip or are part of a tour package, find out if there are any discounts or special deals available. For bigger parties, many resorts and activity providers provide discounts.

Use free Wi-Fi access in hotels, cafés, and public spaces to stay connected and save money on cell data fees: Keep your connection active and access the web without spending more money.

Schedule direct flights: To minimize layovers and unnecessary travel costs, if feasible, schedule direct flights to the Maldives. Direct flights may save you time and money and are often more convenient.

Check whether there are any local events or festivals taking place during your stay by doing some research on them: These ethnic events often provide unique encounters and entertainment, sometimes without extra expense.

In summary, going to the Maldives doesn't have to be expensive. You can take in the splendor of this tropical paradise while controlling your costs if you use these 20 money-saving suggestions. You can enjoy a wonderful vacation in the Maldives without breaking the bank by picking up budget-friendly lodgings, experiencing local food, and taking advantage of free activities. Remember that what counts are your experiences and memories;

with good preparation, you may make them without going overboard.

CHAPTER 3

GETTING AROUND MALDIVES

Once you are familiar with the numerous modes of transportation, getting about this tropical paradise is rather simple. The several methods to visit and experience the Maldives will be covered in this book.

Domestic Flights: Your first move after landing at the Malé International Airport will probably be to board a domestic flight to your vacation island or other location. There are multiple domestic airports in the Maldives, and various local airlines provide frequent service. In comparison to other forms of transportation, these airlines provide simple connections to a variety of atolls. Domestic flights are dependable and pleasant, and they provide breathtaking vantage points of the dispersed islands.

Speedboats: For shorter trips, such as transfers between Malé and surrounding resort islands or neighboring islands, speedboats are a common means of transportation.

It is a hassle-free choice since many resorts organize speedboat transports for their visitors. For those wanting more flexibility and privacy, private speedboat charters is also an option. You may take in the lovely surroundings as you cruise over the crystal-clear waters in one of the speedboats' comfy seats.

Ferries: In the Maldives, ferries are a practical and genuine means to get between small islands. Public ferries are run by the Maldives Transport and Contracting Company (MTCC) to link different atolls and islands.

Both residents and visitors utilize these boats, giving you the chance to meet the kind, Maldivian people. The boat excursions may take longer than other forms of transportation, but they provide a cost-effective choice for tourists who wish to visit other islands and learn about the local way of life.

Seaplanes: Seaplanes are a great option for people looking for an extraordinary and breathtaking experience. Seaplane services are offered from Malé International Airport to private island resorts. You may experience the breathtaking aerial views of the atolls, blue lagoons, and coral reefs by taking a seaplane flight. Trans Maldivian Airways (TMA) and Maldivian Air Taxi (MAT) both offer seaplanes, which are practical and effective means of getting to your destination swiftly.

Dhonis: For decades, people have traveled across the Maldives using these ancient boats, known as dhonis. These sail- or motor-powered wooden boats were historically used for transit between islands and for fishing. Today, a lot of resorts offer dhoni excursions and sunset sails so you may enjoy the Maldivian maritime history. Dhoni excursions give a quiet, unhurried approach to seeing the beauty of the archipelago, floating over the tranquil seas, and providing possibilities for snorkeling and dolphin viewing.

Private yachts and cruises are available for rent in the Maldives if you're looking for a lavish and opulent experience. With this choice, you are given the freedom to take your time discovering the many atolls.

Private yachts have a crew, guaranteeing a smooth and opulent ride. You may appreciate the seclusion of your own floating villa, go to uninhabited islands, scuba dive in pristine coral reefs, and experience the Maldives in the lap of luxury.

In conclusion, traveling in the Maldives is a pleasure with a variety of modes of transportation accessible to meet all tastes and price ranges. Every method of transportation, including domestic aircraft, speedboats, ferries, seaplanes, dhonis, and private yachts, gives a distinctive viewpoint and enables you to fully appreciate this tropical paradise.

Prepare to discover the Maldives' beautiful islands, blue oceans, and abundant marine life.

HOW TO GET FROM MALDIVES AIRPORT TO MALDIVES CITY CENTER

Travelers often need to make their way to the city center after landing at Maldives Airport (formally known as Velana International Airport) to see the dynamic capital, Malé. In this guide, we'll give you a thorough breakdown of the several modes of transportation you may use to go from the Maldives Airport to the city center.

First choice: Public Ferry

Taking a public boat is one of the most convenient and beautiful methods to get to Maldives City Center. As soon as you leave the airport, go to the nearby ferry station. Between Malé and Hulhulé Island, where the airport is located, there are frequent boat services. The trip takes around 15 minutes and provides spectacular views of the blue seas nearby. It's a good idea to double-verify the times in advance since ferry timetables might change. Because the fares are affordable, it is a desirable choice for tourists on a tight budget.

Option 2: Transfer by speedboat

The Maldives Airport offers speedboat services for those seeking a more rapid and practical journey. Several private businesses provide speedboat rides from the airport to Malé. Since they run on a set timetable, these services are often quicker than the regular boat, taking just around 10 minutes to get to the city center. Although speedboat transfers are more costly than ferry transfers, they provide a convenient and pleasant mode of transportation, particularly if you have a lot of baggage or a limited amount of time.

Third Choice: Private Transfer

Setting up a private transfer is a great choice if you desire a customized and hassle-free transfer. In the Maldives, a lot of resorts and hotels provide private shuttle services, including airport pickups. These transfers often combine a quick shuttle trip from the airport to a close-by dock with a speedboat service that takes you straight to your destination in Malé. Despite being more costly than other choices, private shuttles provide comfort, privacy, and a smooth ride to the city core.

4th choice: taxi services

Taxis are easily accessible outside the airport terminal and provide a quick way to get into the city. The majority of the cabs in the Maldives are yellow, and they carry a "Taxi" sign on the top. Taxis provide a door-to-door service, although they are sometimes more costly than choices. Before beginning the voyage, it is important to haggle and reach an agreement on a fee. Depending on traffic, taxi travel from the Maldives Airport to Malé takes around 15 minutes.

Option 5: Shuttle service to the airport

In the Maldives, a few resorts and hotels offer their visitors free airport shuttle services. Check to see whether a hotel or resort offers a shuttle service if you have a reservation there. These services often entail a shuttle bus or van that transports you from the airport to a local dock from whence, depending on where your hotel is located, you may take a ferry or a speedboat to go to your destination in Malé.

To accommodate a variety of tastes and budgets, there are several transportation choices available for getting from the Maldives Airport to the Maldives City Center.

You may effectively and easily get to the dynamic capital, Malé, whether you choose the gorgeous public ferry, the quick speedboat, the convenience of private transport, a taxi trip, or an airport shuttle service.

Choose the choice that best suits your requirements and have pleasure in your voyage to the Maldives by keeping in mind your priorities, such as cost, trip duration, and degree of luxury.

HOW TO GET FROM MALDIVES AIRPORT TO THE NEAREST HOTELS

The country's well-developed transportation system makes it reasonably simple to go from the Maldives Airport to the closest hotels. The principal international entrance to the Maldives, an archipelago in the Indian Ocean, is Velana International Airport, sometimes called Malé International Airport (MLE). An explanation of how to get from the airport to the nearby hotels is provided below:

When you arrive at Velana International Airport: you will exit from your aircraft and go through immigration and customs. Before going to the arrivals area, make sure to get your bags.

Options for transportation: There are a few ways to go from the airport to your accommodation. These consist of:

A lot of resorts and hotels in the Maldives provide speedboat rides from the airport to their specific locations. Usually, these transportation services are pre-planned and included in the hotel rate. You will be met by the hotel staff as you leave the arrivals area, and they will direct you to the location of the speedboat departure.

Domestic flights: You may need to take a domestic flight if your hotel is on a separate island from the airport. The Domestic

Terminal, which is close to the international terminal, is where domestic planes take off and land. Follow the directions to the domestic terminal after leaving the international terminal. Before boarding your domestic aircraft, you must check in and go through security. Depending on your destination, the length of your trip to another island may change.

Seaplane transports: Because certain resorts and hotels are situated on far-flung islands, these transfers may be necessary. A gorgeous and distinctive way to get to your accommodation, seaplanes let you take in breathtaking aerial views of the Maldivian islands. A separate terminal close to the airport is where seaplanes are operated. You must go on to the seaplane terminal to check in for your flight after leaving the international terminal.

The management of transportation is something that many hotels in the Maldives take care of for their visitors. You should speak with your hotel in advance to clarify the available transport choices and any special instructions they may have.

On their websites or in interactions with guests before their arrival, hotels often provide comprehensive information about their transportation services.

Tips and considerations:

There are airport kiosks and travel agencies in the arrivals area where you may make last-minute transfer arrangements if you haven't already done so with your hotel.

Check the schedules for domestic flights and seaplanes in advance since they could only operate during certain hours.

It is advised to bring essentials in your carry-on bag in case your checked baggage is delayed during transit, such as prescriptions or a change of clothing.

If you arrive late at night or have a lengthy stopover, you may choose to stay the night at a hotel close to the airport before continuing the next day to your ultimate destination.

You should enjoy a simple and easy trip from the Maldives Airport to the closest hotels by following these instructions and taking into account the supplied advice. Enjoy your stay in this oasis of the tropics!

PUBLIC WIFI AVAILABILITY IN MALDIVES

Even while it could appear like a place to disengage from technology and immerse oneself in the natural beauty, many tourists nonetheless place high importance on being connected. To help you remain connected while on your ideal holiday, this travel guide strives to give comprehensive information regarding the accessibility and availability of free WiFi in the Maldives.

An Overview of Maldives' Internet Connectivity

In recent years, internet access in the Maldives has substantially improved, particularly on resort islands and in high-traffic tourist regions. Despite the country's many isolated islands, efforts have been undertaken to build a solid internet infrastructure to meet the rising demand of both visitors and people. Broadband and satellite connections are the Maldives' primary sources of internet access.

Resorts and Hotels: The majority of resorts and hotels in the Maldives provide WiFi connections to their visitors. You'll probably have access to free WiFi at your lodging whether you're in a posh overwater villa or a modest guesthouse. While some upscale resorts provide high-speed internet access without charge, others can levy a surcharge for a premium connection.

Public Places: Public WiFi hotspots are available in major urban areas and tourist hotspots like Male, the nation's capital, and other populated islands.

These consist of coffee shops, restaurants, retail centers, and well-known tourist destinations. Even though the speed and dependability of public WiFi might change, you can connect to it with your smartphone, tablet, or laptop and it's often free to use.

Airports: Velana International Airport (MLE), the principal international airport serving the Maldives, offers free WiFi access in all of its terminals. This enables tourists to maintain contact while awaiting their flights or while using the transportation system. In airport terminals, the WiFi network name and password are often posted, making connection simple.

SIM Cards & Mobile Data: Buying a local SIM card is a great choice if you want constant internet access during your vacation. The Maldives has several telecommunications service providers, including Dhiraagu and Ooredoo. You may purchase SIM cards at their airport kiosks, neighborhood businesses, or their respective official retailers.

Once you have a local SIM card, you may choose the data package that best meets your requirements from a variety of options. These plans often include high-speed 4G LTE access, enabling you to utilize VoIP services like WhatsApp and Skype to make calls as well as surf the internet and use social media.

Check with your lodging: Before your vacation, ask your selected resort or hotel about their WiFi availability, fees (if any), and the regions served by the WiFi network.

International roaming fees and data roaming: If you choose not to buy a local SIM card, be aware that these fees might be quite high.

To learn about prices and available data plans, speak with your cell service provider.

Offline maps and applications: Before your journey, download offline maps and practical travel apps to reduce the need for continual internet access. By doing so, you can go about the islands and get important information without depending only on an internet connection.

Respect local traditions and laws: When using mobile data or public WiFi, be aware of local laws and refrain from viewing or transmitting inappropriate information. Like any other nation, the Maldives has its own set of guidelines for using the Internet.

As a result of the expansion of public WiFi hotspots, resort connection, and the availability of local SIM cards, staying connected while vacationing in the Maldives is now simpler than ever. If you're expressing your

CHAPTER 4

WHAT YOU NEED TO PACK ON A TRIP TO MALDIVES

It's vital to pack properly to ensure you have everything you need for a comfortable and happy trip. The Maldives is recognized for its gorgeous beaches, crystal-clear seas, and plentiful marine life, so bringing the proper products will improve your experience. Here is a complete and well-explained list of things you need to pack for your vacation to the Maldives:

Lightweight and breathable clothing: The Maldives has a tropical environment with warm temperatures throughout the year. Pack lightweight and breathable apparel such as shorts, sundresses, t-shirts, and swimwear. Opt for light, natural textiles like cotton and linen to keep cool and comfortable in the humid heat.

Sun protection essentials: The sun in the Maldives can be extremely harsh, so be sure to carry the necessary goods for sun protection. Include sunscreen with a high SPF, sunglasses, a wide-brimmed hat, and a sarong or cover-up to shelter yourself from the sun's rays. It's also a good idea to have a rash guard or long-sleeved shirt for added protection when swimming or snorkeling.

Snorkeling gear: The Maldives is famous for its magnificent coral reefs and plentiful marine life, making snorkeling a popular sport.

Consider bringing your snorkeling gear, including a mask, snorkel, and fins, to have the flexibility to explore the underwater environment at your leisure. While some resorts may supply equipment, having your own assures a great fit and cleanliness.

Underwater camera: With its magnificent marine life, the Maldives provides lots of options for underwater photography. Invest in a good-quality underwater camera or a waterproof casing for your current camera to record the vivid coral reefs, colorful fish, and possibly even dolphins or turtles you may see on your snorkeling or diving experiences.

Water shoes or sandals: Some of the beaches in the Maldives feature coral and jagged rocks, so it's suggested to take water shoes or strong sandals to protect your feet while entering the sea. These will also come in useful for exploring tidal pools or wandering on sandy beaches.

Prescriptions and basic first aid kit: It's always advisable to bring vital prescriptions and a basic first aid kit while traveling. Include goods like pain remedies, antihistamines, band-aids, antiseptic creams, and any prescription prescriptions you may need. While resorts and local pharmacies are accessible, it's essential to have your required supplies on hand.

Insect repellent: Mosquitoes and other insects might be prevalent in some locations of the Maldives, particularly during the evening. To protect yourself from bites and dangerous infections, bring a high-quality insect repellent containing DEET or similar efficient components.

Travel adapters and chargers: The Maldives employs Type G electrical outlets, therefore if your gadgets have various plug types, be sure you carry suitable travel adapters. Don't forget to carry chargers for your electrical gadgets such as cameras, phones, and computers to keep them charged during your vacation.

Travel paperwork and copies: Ensure you have all relevant travel documents such as your passport, aircraft tickets, hotel bookings, and travel insurance data. It's a good idea to create digital copies and retain physical copies as well, as it might be handy in case of any unanticipated occurrences.

Reusable water bottle: Staying hydrated is crucial, particularly in a tropical climate. Pack a reusable water bottle to prevent plastic waste and refill it with bottled water or filtered water available during your stay. Remember to remain hydrated, particularly while spending time under the sun or indulging in outdoor activities.

Cash and cards: While credit cards are generally accepted in resorts and tourist areas, it's good to carry some cash for little transactions in case you discover establishments that only take cash. Ensure you contact your bank about your vacation intentions to prevent any card complications while overseas.

Travel insurance: It's strongly suggested to get travel insurance that covers medical emergencies, trip cancellations, and lost or stolen possessions. Review your policy before your travel to understand what is covered and maintain a copy of your insurance documentation conveniently available.

Remember to travel light and prioritize goods that are important for your comfort and pleasure in the Maldives. By considering the tropical environment, outdoor activities, and the need for sun protection, you can assure a well-prepared and pleasurable journey to this lovely place.

CHAPTER 5

TOP TOURIST DESTINATIONS IN MALDIVES

The Maldives has become a dream location for vacationers seeking a calm and picturesque retreat. In this post, we will examine 20 of the finest tourist locations in the Maldives, each delivering a distinct experience that will leave you enthralled.

Malé: The capital city of Maldives, Malé, is a dynamic and busy metropolis where the bulk of the local population dwells. While it may lack the gorgeous beaches, it gives a true peek into Maldivian culture, with its colorful marketplaces, historical sites, and lively fish market.

Hulhumalé: Located near Malé, Hulhumalé is a manmade island famed for its magnificent beaches and sophisticated infrastructure. This up-and-coming resort provides a choice of activities such as water sports, beach leisure, and eco-parks.

Maafushi: Maafushi is a local island that has acquired favor among budget vacationers. It provides inexpensive lodgings, scenic beaches, and chances for snorkeling, diving, and water sports.

Biyadhoo Island: Biyadhoo Island, known as the "Island of Scuba Diving," is a diver's paradise. Surrounded by bright coral reefs, it provides great diving and snorkeling possibilities, enabling tourists to explore the spectacular underwater environment.

Bandos Island: Bandos Island is recognized for its picture-perfect beaches and rich nature. It has magnificent resorts, water sports activities, and a thriving marine ecology that may be explored via snorkeling or diving.

Addu Atoll: Located in the southernmost portion of the Maldives, Addu Atoll is a group of islands famed for its clean beaches, vivid coral reefs, and plentiful marine life. It provides a variety of activities such as cycling, kayaking, and visiting historical places.

Baa Atoll: Baa Atoll is a UNESCO Biosphere Reserve and a refuge for environment aficionados. It features great wildlife, including manta rays and whale sharks. Visitors may enjoy diving, snorkeling, and guided excursions to view the beautiful aquatic life.

Vaadhoo Island: Vaadhoo Island is famed for its unique natural phenomenon known as bioluminescence. At night, the beaches light up with a stunning blue glow generated by bioluminescent plankton, providing an unearthly experience.

Alimatha Island: Alimatha Island is located in the Vaavu Atoll and is recognized for its flourishing marine life and world-class diving locations. The island provides a multitude of water activities, including snorkeling, diving, and night fishing.

Mirihi Island: Mirihi Island is a tiny, private paradise with beautiful beaches and magnificent resorts. It is great for honeymooners and anyone seeking a romantic vacation. The island provides a quiet ambiance, and good snorkeling, and diving chances.

Fihalhohi Island: Fihalhohi Island is a tropical paradise surrounded by crystal-clear seas and beautiful coral reefs. It provides a multitude of aquatic sports, including snorkeling, diving, and fishing. The island also offers a calm setting for leisure.

Vilamendhoo Island: Vilamendhoo Island is recognized for its gorgeous house reef, making it popular among snorkelers and divers. The island provides a laid-back ambiance, magnificent beaches, and a multitude of water sports activities.

Veligandu Island: Veligandu Island is a tiny, quiet sanctuary famed for its gorgeous beaches and blue lagoon. The island provides exquisite lodgings, water activities, and a spa for maximum relaxation.

Kuredu Island: Kuredu Island is one of the major resort islands in the Maldives and provides a broad choice of activities and services.

It has gorgeous beaches, rich marine life, golfing, tennis, and numerous water sports.

Dhigurah Island: Dhigurah Island is noted for its pure white-sand beaches and being a gateway to swimming with whale sharks. The island offers a tranquil and serene setting for relaxing, along with options for diving and snorkeling.

Ari Atoll: Ari Atoll is recognized for its opulent resorts, gorgeous coral reefs, and colorful marine life. It provides a wonderful combination of leisure and excitement, with activities like diving, snorkeling, and fishing.

Rasdhoo Island: Rasdhoo Island is a paradise for snorkeling and diving aficionados, with its near vicinity to the famed Hammerhead Shark Point. The island also provides stunning beaches and an opportunity to immerse yourself in the native culture.

Thoddoo Island: Thoddoo Island is noted for its booming agricultural business, notably its enormous fields of juicy watermelons. Visitors may explore the island's fruit farms, enjoy water sports activities, and rest on its calm beaches.

Utheemu Island: Utheemu Island possesses historical importance as the birthplace of Sultan Mohamed Thakurufaanu, a national hero. Visitors may visit the old Utheemu Ganduvaru, a wooden palace, and learn about the Maldives' rich cultural legacy.

Banana Reef: Banana Reef is a renowned diving location, famed for its unusual banana-like form and rich marine life. Divers may view a variety of fish species, coral formations, and even reef sharks, making it a must-visit site for diving aficionados.

Conclusion: The Maldives really fulfills the image of a tropical paradise, delivering spectacular natural beauty, excellent lodgings, and a multitude of water sports activities. From the beautiful beaches and bright coral reefs to the rich cultural legacy and warm hospitality of the inhabitants, the Maldives is a location that offers an amazing experience for everyone who comes. Whether you desire leisure, adventure, or a romantic break, these top 20 tourist sites in the Maldives offer a great blend of natural beauty and opulent comforts.

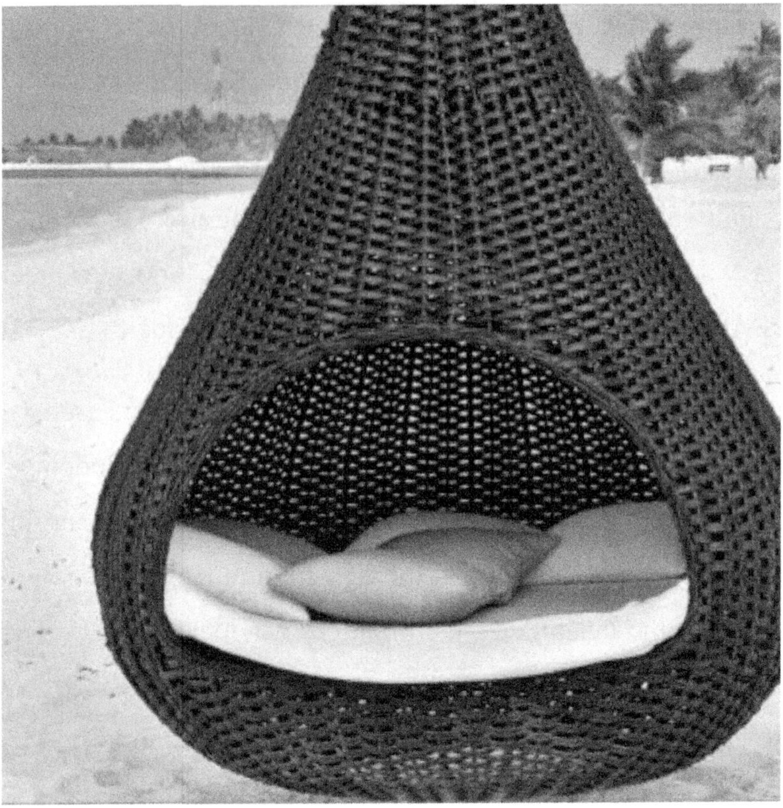

CHAPTER 6

BEST BEACHES IN MALDIVES

The Maldives, an archipelago of 26 coral atolls located in the Indian Ocean, is famous for its magnificent natural beauty and clean beaches. With crystal-clear blue seas, pure white beaches, and rich marine life, the Maldives is an ideal vacation for beach lovers and sunseekers. In this post, we will examine the 20 greatest beaches in the Maldives, providing a look into the magical splendor of this tropical paradise.

Veligandu Island Beach: Located in the North Ari Atoll, Veligandu Island Beach is an isolated piece of heaven. Its powdery soft beach, swaying palm trees, and blue seas provide a picture-perfect environment. Snorkeling and diving aficionados will be pleased by the vibrant coral reefs abounding with marine life.

Cocoa Island Beach: Cocoa Island Beach, located in the South Malé Atoll, is famed for its pure white beaches and turquoise seas. This beach provides privacy and tranquillity, making it a great destination for honeymooners and those seeking a romantic retreat.

Reethi Beach: Reethi Beach, situated on Baa Atoll, is famed for its lush flora, silky beaches, and rich marine life. Snorkeling in its crystal-clear lagoon is a must-do activity here, as it enables you to discover the rich underwater world of the Maldives.

Fulhadhoo Beach: Fulhadhoo Beach, on Fulhadhoo Island, features a magnificent coral reef only meters away from its shoreline. The beach provides a real Maldivian experience with its pristine beauty and tranquil environment.

Hulhumale Beach: Hulhumale Beach, located on Hulhumale Island in Malé, is a popular beach among residents and visitors alike. It provides a handy respite for people living in the capital city and gives spectacular views of the sunset.

Fihalhohi Island Beach: Fihalhohi Island Beach, situated in the South Malé Atoll, is a sanctuary for beach lovers. The island is surrounded by a colorful coral reef, making it a perfect site for snorkeling and diving experiences.

Baros Island Beach: Baros Island Beach, tucked in the North Malé Atoll, is famed for its crystal-clear seas and pure white sand. The beach is bordered by a house reef, which provides great snorkeling and diving possibilities.

Biyadhoo Island Beach: Biyadhoo Island Beach, located in the South Malé Atoll, is a haven for nature aficionados. Its palm-fringed coastlines, lush foliage, and rich marine life make it a favorite option for snorkelers and divers.

Maafushi Island Beach: Maafushi Island Beach, situated in Kaafu Atoll, is a favorite location for budget vacationers. It boasts a lovely beach with pristine seas, and tourists may also enjoy a selection of water sports and excursions from this vibrant island.

Nalaguraidhoo Beach: Nalaguraidhoo Beach, located in South Ari Atoll, is home to some of the greatest diving areas in the Maldives. The beach has pristine white beaches, crystal-clear seas, and a variety of colorful marine life.

Vabbinfaru Island Beach: Vabbinfaru Island Beach, situated in North Malé Atoll, is recognized for its scenic beauty and solitude. The beach provides a calm ambiance and is great for a romantic stroll along the coast.

Ukulhas Island Beach: Ukulhas Island Beach, located in North Ari Atoll, is noted for its pure seas and spectacular coral reefs. The beach is also noted for its eco-friendly efforts, making it a fantastic option for concerned vacationers.

Mirihi Island Beach: Mirihi Island Beach, situated in South Ari Atoll, provides a postcard-perfect environment with its pristine white beaches and blue seas. The beach is great for leisure, snorkeling, and watching spectacular sunsets.

Maafushivaru Island Beach: Maafushivaru Island Beach, located in South Ari Atoll, is a secluded beach recognized for its luxury resorts and unspoiled beauty. It provides the ideal hideaway for individuals seeking seclusion and exclusivity.

Velassaru Island Beach: Velassaru Island Beach, situated in South Malé Atoll, is a paradise for water sports aficionados. With its tranquil seas and plentiful marine life, it provides great chances for snorkeling, diving, and kayaking.

Dhigurah Island Beach: Dhigurah Island Beach, located in South Ari Atoll, is noted for its long length of pure white sand and crystal-clear seas. It is also noted for its regular sightings of whale sharks, making it a favorite location for marine aficionados.

Thulusdhoo Island Beach: Thulusdhoo Island Beach, situated in North Malé Atoll, is a notable surf destination in the Maldives. Surfers go to this beach to ride its legendary left-hand surf break known as "Cokes."

Dhuni Kolhu Island Beach: Dhuni Kolhu Island Beach, located in Baa Atoll, is noted for its pristine beauty and luxurious resorts. The beach provides a tranquil getaway surrounded by lush flora and spectacular aquatic life.

Rangali Island Beach: Rangali Island Beach, situated in South Ari Atoll, is home to the magnificent Conrad Maldives Rangali Island resort. The beach features smooth beaches, clean seas, and an underwater restaurant, delivering a completely unique eating experience.

Thoddoo Island Beach: Thoddoo Island Beach, located in Alif Alif Atoll, is recognized for its gorgeous sceneries and extensive fruit orchards. The beach provides a calm respite with its blue seas and waving palm palms.

Conclusion: The Maldives is a tropical paradise that captivates travelers with its gorgeous beaches and magnificent natural beauty. Whether you desire leisure, adventure, or romance, the 20 greatest beaches in the Maldives provide a broad selection of experiences to fit any traveler's interests. From immaculate white sands to vivid coral reefs, these beaches give an incredible look into the picturesque beauty of this fascinating region.

BEST RESTAURANTS IN MALDIVES

the eateries in this tropical paradise deliver a gourmet adventure like no other. In this post, we will examine the 20 greatest restaurants in the Maldives, displaying their distinct products, breathtaking settings, and excellent dining experiences.

Ithaa Undersea Restaurant (Rangali Island): Immerse yourself in a genuinely remarkable experience at Ithaa Undersea Restaurant, positioned five meters below the water's surface. Enjoy panoramic views of the vivid marine life while eating a tasty combination of Western and Asian cuisine.

Sea.Fire.Salt (Huvafen Fushi): Situated on a private island, Sea.Fire.Salt provides a stunning overwater environment. Indulge in a choice of gourmet meals cooked with the freshest seafood, quality pieces of meat, and a variety of delicious salts from around the globe.

5.8 Undersea Restaurant (Niyama Private Islands): Dine five meters below the ocean's surface at 5.8 Undersea Restaurant, surrounded by magnificent coral reefs. The cuisine presents a mix of tastes, accompanied by an extensive wine list, providing for an exciting gastronomic adventure.

The Lighthouse (Gili Lankanfushi): Perched above the turquoise waves, The Lighthouse provides a magnificent backdrop and a menu that honors world cuisine. Enjoy a broad choice of foods, from fresh seafood to gourmet meat cuts, while enjoying breathtaking panoramic views.

Alizée (Dusit Thani Maldives): Alizée offers beautiful beachside views with food influenced by the Mediterranean and beyond. Savor delectable seafood, grilled meats, and savory salads, all made with the greatest ingredients and culinary skill.

Ufaa by Jereme Leung (The Ritz-Carlton Maldives, Fari Islands): Experience the art of contemporary Chinese cuisine at Ufaa, guided by renowned chef Jereme Leung. The restaurant exhibits a distinct combination of tastes, blending traditional Chinese methods with locally obtained products.

Reef Club (Coco Bodu Hithi): Located on a private island, Reef Club provides an exquisite seaside environment. Indulge in a range of different cuisines, including fresh seafood, sushi, and Mediterranean-inspired meals, while enjoying the relaxing coastal wind.

Feeling Koi (Soneva Jani): Nestled over the turquoise lagoon, Feeling Koi delivers delicious Japanese cuisine with a twist. Enjoy a unique cuisine with sushi, sashimi, and robata-grilled foods, complemented by handmade beverages and magnificent sunset views.

The Wine Cellar (Kuramathi Maldives): Wine connoisseurs will rejoice at The Wine Cellar, presenting a vast range of wines from throughout the globe. Enjoy wine tastings, combined with delicious cheeses and cold cuts, in a unique subterranean atmosphere.

Aqua (Four Seasons Resort Maldives in Landaa Giraavaru): Aqua features a spectacular beachside location with a menu highlighting fresh seafood and Italian cuisine. The wood-fired pizzas and handmade pasta dishes are complimented by an exceptional wine selection.

Underwater Restaurant (Hurawalhi Island Resort): Immerse yourself in a gourmet journey in the world's biggest all-glass underwater restaurant. Indulge in a delectable multi-course feast while gazing at the beautiful marine creatures swimming past.

Tribal (Naladhu Private Island): Tribal provides an intimate dining experience nestled on a private beach. The cuisine contains a blend of Asian and African ingredients, providing a unique and fascinating gastronomic adventure.

The Falhumaa (Coco Palm Dhuni Kolhu): Situated on a secluded island, The Falhumaa provides a romantic setting with stunning ocean views. The menu features world cuisine, with a focus on fresh seafood and Maldivian delicacies.

Samsara Asian Fusion (OZEN Reserve Bolifushi): Samsara Asian Fusion delivers a lively combination of Asian tastes and modern cuisine. The restaurant provides a range of culinary genres, including Chinese, Thai, Japanese, and Indian, assuring a great eating experience.

Muraka (Conrad Maldives Rangali Island): Muraka, a unique underwater restaurant, and apartment brings luxury dining to new depths. Delight in an exceptional tasting cuisine while surrounded by captivating aquatic life, offering a unique sensory experience.

By the Beach (Kanuhura Maldives): Experience a casual dining occasion with your toes on the beach at By the Beach. The restaurant delivers a delightful combination of Mediterranean, Asian, and Maldivian foods, complimented by spectacular sunset views.

Reethi Grill (Reethi Beach Resort): Reethi Grill provides a stunning beachside setting and intriguing grill cuisine. Feast on freshly caught fish, luscious meats, and scrumptious vegetarian alternatives while enjoying the tranquil ambiance.

Baan Huraa (Four Seasons Resort Maldives at Kuda Huraa): Baan Huraa takes visitors to Thailand with its genuine Thai cuisine and exquisite beachfront surroundings. Delight in a broad choice of traditional foods created by professional Thai cooks.

Origami (Kandima Maldives): Origami combines the finest of Japanese cuisine with a modern twist. Savor sushi, sashimi, and other Japanese delicacies while taking in panoramic views of the island's natural splendor.

Faru (Hurawalhi Island Resort): Faru provides a romantic, overwater dining experience with breathtaking sunset views. The menu provides a diversity of foreign cuisines, including fresh seafood, grilled meats, and vegetarian alternatives.

Conclusion: The Maldives' food scene is a harmonic blend of world-class cuisine, gorgeous locations, and exceptional dining experiences. From underwater restaurants to beachside grills, these 20 top restaurants illustrate the range and excellence of cuisine offered in this tropical paradise.

Whether you're a seafood fanatic, a fan of Asian cuisine, or seeking a romantic ambiance, the Maldives offers a restaurant to please every pallet. Indulge in the pleasures of this gorgeous region, and let your taste buds embark on a gourmet adventure like no other.

BUDGET-FRIENDLY HOTELS TO STAY

there are some budget-friendly hotels that provide a terrific experience without breaking the bank. In this post, we give a selection of 20 budget hotels in the Maldives that provide comfortable accommodations, magnificent views, and access to the great beauty of the islands.

Rashu Hiyaa, Dhiffushi Island: Located on Dhiffushi Island, Rashu Hiyaa provides pleasant rooms with contemporary facilities, including air conditioning, private bathrooms, and complimentary Wi-Fi. The hotel has a rooftop patio with magnificent views of the Indian Ocean and a restaurant offering local and foreign cuisine.

Salt Beach Hotel, Maafushi Island: Situated on Maafushi Island, Salt Beach Hotel has spacious rooms equipped with air conditioning, flat-screen TVs, and private bathrooms. Guests may enjoy the hotel's outdoor swimming pool, sun deck, and an on-site restaurant offering great seafood.

Island Cottage, Guraidhoo Island: Island Cottage is a beautiful guesthouse on Guraidhoo Island, providing cheap rooms with air conditioning, private bathrooms, and free Wi-Fi. The resort offers a garden, a communal sitting space, and a restaurant offering Maldivian and Western food.

Koimala Hotel, Gulhi Island: Nestled on Gulhi Island, Koimala Hotel provides comfortable accommodations with air conditioning, private bathrooms, and free amenities. The hotel has a restaurant, a communal lounge, and a 24-hour front desk.

Canopus Retreat Thulusdhoo, Thulusdhoo Island: Canopus Retreat Thulusdhoo is situated on Thulusdhoo Island and provides well-appointed rooms with air conditioning, private bathrooms, and complimentary Wi-Fi. Guests may enjoy the hotel's garden, patio, and an on-site restaurant.

Cokes Surf Camp, Thulusdhoo Island: Ideal for surf aficionados, Cokes Surf Camp on Thulusdhoo Island provides budget-friendly accommodation with air conditioning, private toilets, and a communal sitting area. The hotel has immediate access to the famed Cokes surf break.

Velana Beach Maldives, Maafushi Island: Velana Beach Maldives, located on Maafushi Island, provides spacious rooms with air conditioning, flat-screen TVs, and private bathrooms. Guests may relax on the hotel's sun deck or enjoy snorkeling and diving excursions offered by the resort.

Planktons Beach Hotel, Hulhumale Island: Planktons Beach Hotel is situated on Hulhumale Island, near Male International Airport. The motel has pleasant rooms with air conditioning, private bathrooms, and complimentary Wi-Fi. Guests may recline on the beachside patio and sample local and international cuisine at the hotel's restaurant.

Bibee Maldives, Maafushi Island: Bibee Maldives is a budget-friendly hotel on Maafushi Island, providing comfortable rooms with air conditioning, private bathrooms, and free Wi-Fi. The motel features bicycle rentals, a garden, and a communal lounge area.

Seashine Maldives, Thoddoo Island: Situated on Thoddoo Island, Seashine Maldives provides cheap rooms with air conditioning, private bathrooms, and a sitting area. The hotel features bicycle rentals, a communal kitchen, and a sun deck for guests to enjoy.

Kaani Village & Spa, Maafushi Island: Kaani Village & Spa, situated on Maafushi Island, provides pleasant rooms equipped with air conditioning, private bathrooms, and complimentary Wi-Fi. The hotel has a spa, a garden, and an on-site restaurant offering a range of cuisines.

Green Shade, Guraidhoo Island: Green Shade is a budget-friendly guesthouse on Guraidhoo Island, providing comfortable rooms with air conditioning, private bathrooms, and free Wi-Fi. The unit features a garden, a patio, and a common sitting area.

Picnic Inn, Guraidhoo Island: Located on Guraidhoo Island, Picnic Inn provides cheap rooms with air conditioning, private bathrooms, and complimentary Wi-Fi. The hotel offers a garden, a sun patio, and a restaurant offering local and foreign foods.

Beachwood Hotel, Hulhumale Island: Beachwood Hotel, located on Hulhumale Island, features spacious rooms with air conditioning, private bathrooms, and complimentary Wi-Fi. Guests may relax on the hotel's balcony, enjoy water sports activities, and eat at the on-site restaurant.

Koamas Lodge, Rasdhoo Island: Koamas Lodge is situated on Rasdhoo Island and provides cheap accommodation with air conditioning, private toilets, and complimentary Wi-Fi. The hotel includes a courtyard, a communal lounge, and a 24-hour front desk.

Arena Lodge Maldives, Hulhumale Island: Situated on Hulhumale Island, Arena Lodge Maldives provides spacious rooms with air conditioning, private bathrooms, and complimentary Wi-Fi. The hotel offers a patio, a communal lounge, and a restaurant offering local and foreign cuisine.

Surf Retreat Maldives, Himmafushi Island: Surf Retreat Maldives, situated on Himmafushi Island, offers cheap accommodation with air conditioning, private bathrooms, and complimentary Wi-Fi. Guests may enjoy the hotel's garden, patio, and an on-site restaurant.

Faza Inn, Maafushi Island: Faza Inn is a budget-friendly hotel on Maafushi Island, providing comfortable rooms with air conditioning, private bathrooms, and complimentary Wi-Fi. The hotel features a garden, a sun patio, and a restaurant offering local and foreign cuisine.

Sandy Heaven Maldives, Maafushi Island: Sandy Heaven Maldives, located on Maafushi Island, provides pleasant rooms equipped with air conditioning, private bathrooms, and complimentary Wi-Fi. The hotel offers a restaurant, a garden, and a sun deck.

Dream Relax Guest House, Maafushi Island: Dream Relax Guest House is situated on Maafushi Island and provides cheap rooms with air conditioning, private bathrooms, and free Wi-Fi. The guesthouse features a garden, a communal lounge, and a restaurant offering a range of meals.

Conclusion: Traveling to the Maldives on a budget is certainly achievable given the large choice of budget-friendly hotels accessible throughout the islands. These 20 hotels provide comfortable lodging, needed facilities, and convenient access to the spectacular beauty of the Maldives. Whether you're wanting to enjoy water sports, relax on the beautiful beaches, or explore the colorful marine life, these budget alternatives enable you to experience the Maldives without breaking the bank.

BEST LUXURY HOTELS TO STAY IN MALDIVES

Renowned for its elite resorts and overwater villas, the Maldives provides an unrivaled degree of luxury and pleasure. In this post, we offer the 20 top luxury hotels in the Maldives that epitomize the ultimate island retreat.

Soneva Jani: Nestled in the Noonu Atoll, Soneva Jani provides the ideal combination of nature and luxury. This resort boasts spectacular overwater villas with private pools and waterslides, open-air baths, and direct access to the crystal-clear lagoon.

Gili Lankanfushi: Situated in the North Malé Atoll, Gili Lankanfushi provides a calm and private experience. The huge overwater villas have private decks, outdoor bathrooms, and direct access to the coral-rich seas.

One&Only Reethi Rah: Located on one of the biggest islands in North Malé Atoll, One&Only Reethi Rah features magnificent villas with private pools, captivating ocean views, and premium facilities like private chefs and personal butlers.

Cheval Blanc Randheli: This magnificent resort in the Noonu Atoll features superbly constructed villas including modern architecture, private infinity pools, and direct access to the pristine beaches. The resort also provides a selection of world-class dining alternatives.

Six Senses Laamu: Secluded on the Laamu Atoll, Six Senses Laamu is an eco-friendly luxury resort that provides sustainable but opulent lodgings. The overwater villas, surrounded by turquoise waves, provide unbroken seclusion and magnificent sunsets.

Four Seasons Resort Maldives at Landaa Giraavaru: Known for its superb service and magnificent location in the Baa Atoll, Four Seasons Landaa Giraavaru provides exquisite beach and overwater villas, a world-class spa, and a renowned marine research center.

COMO Maalifushi: Situated in the isolated Thaa Atoll, COMO Maalifushi exhibits spectacular overwater villas and beach suites with private pools. Guests may engage in holistic health treatments, enjoy water sports, or explore the colorful marine life.

Velaa Private Island: A sanctuary of tranquillity in the Noonu Atoll, Velaa Private Island features magnificent villas and houses with private pools, a private beach, and customized butler service. The resort also has a golf school and a submersible for underwater exploration.

Joali Maldives: Located on Muravandhoo Island in the Raa Atoll, Joali Maldives provides exquisite villas and homes constructed by famous artists. The resort promises an immersive experience with curated art exhibits, a spa, and outstanding culinary choices.

Naladhu Private Island Maldives: A hidden haven in the South Malé Atoll, Naladhu Private Island provides exquisite and large villas with private pools, exclusive butler service, and access to a pristine beach. Guests may also enjoy personalized dining experiences and revitalizing spa treatments.

St. Regis Maldives Vommuli Resort: Perched on the Dhaalu Atoll, St. Regis Maldives Vommuli Resort features magnificent overwater and beach villas with private pools. The resort has a champagne bar, a world-class spa, and a private boat for excursions.

Milaidhoo Island Maldives: Nestled in the UNESCO Biosphere Reserve of Baa Atoll, Milaidhoo Island provides exquisite thatched-roof villas with private pools, an open-air bathroom design, and stunning ocean views. The resort also delivers bespoke experiences such as snorkeling with manta rays.

Waldorf Astoria Maldives Ithaafushi: Situated in the South Malé Atoll, Waldorf Astoria Maldives Ithaafushi features magnificent villas and apartments, each with a private pool. Guests may relish gastronomic pleasures at a range of world-class restaurants and luxuriate spa treatments in overwater villas.

Anantara Kihavah Maldives Villas: Set in the Baa Atoll, Anantara Kihavah Maldives Villas provides large villas and homes with private pools, vast sundecks, and spectacular Indian Ocean panoramas. The resort also has an underwater restaurant and a sky observatory.

Kanuhura Maldives: Situated in the Lhaviyani Atoll, Kanuhura Maldives provides luxury beach and overwater villas, each with its own private pool. The resort includes a selection of culinary options, a fantastic spa, and thrilling activities like diving and dolphin excursions.

Amilla Fushi: Located in the UNESCO Biosphere Reserve of Baa Atoll, Amilla Fushi provides a choice of big and elegant villas and homes, including treehouses and beach residences. The resort boasts a private marine biology school, numerous culinary choices, and an opulent spa.

Conrad Maldives Rangali Island: Renowned for its distinctive underwater restaurant, Conrad Maldives Rangali Island provides exquisite beach and water villas with private pools and breathtaking views. Guests may enjoy a multitude of activities, including snorkeling, diving, and sunset cruises.

Huvafen Fushi Maldives: Tucked away in the North Malé Atoll, Huvafen Fushi Maldives provides ultra-luxurious villas and pavilions with private pools, outdoor rain showers, and direct beach or lagoon access. The hotel has the first underwater spa in the world.

Taj Exotica Resort & Spa Maldives: Situated in the South Malé Atoll, Taj Exotica Resort & Spa Maldives offers a tranquil and private setting. The resort provides beautiful villas with private pools, world-class dining choices, and a spa nestled within lush grounds.

Jumeirah Vittaveli: Located in the South Malé Atoll, Jumeirah Vittaveli provides exquisite beach and overwater homes with private pools and direct access to the beautiful beach. The resort includes superb dining choices, an award-winning spa, and an abundance of recreational activities.

Conclusion: The Maldives is a tropical paradise that draws luxury guests with its magnificent beauty and world-class hospitality. The 20 luxury hotels listed in this article offer unmatched experiences, from overwater villas and private pools to excellent cuisine and special spa treatments. Whether you desire seclusion, adventure, or just a chance to relax in unsurpassed luxury, these hotels offer the ideal setting for a memorable Maldivian trip.

BEST SHOPPING MALLS IN MALDIVES

The Maldives features various contemporary retail complexes that appeal to both residents and visitors. In this post, we will examine the 20 greatest shopping malls in the Maldives, providing a mix of retail establishments, leisure alternatives, and culinary experiences.

The Marina at Crossroads: Situated in Male, the capital city of the Maldives, The Marina @ Crossroads is a bustling lifestyle destination that mixes luxury shopping, dining, and entertainment. This retail mall provides a selection of worldwide brands, local shops, and gourmet eateries, making it a must-visit location.

Maldives Islamic Centre: Located in Male, the Maldives Islamic Centre is not only a religious facility but also has a retail arcade.

Here, travelers may discover a variety of boutiques providing apparel, accessories, and souvenirs. The institution also offers cultural exhibits and activities.

Majeedhee Magu: Majeedhee Magu, a lively street in Male, is a major retail area for residents and visitors alike. This busy retail neighborhood includes a mix of stores, boutiques, and booths offering apparel, gadgets, cosmetics, and souvenirs, creating a unique shopping experience.

Orchid Magu: Adjacent to Majeedhee Magu, Orchid Magu is another popular shopping strip with a broad selection of retailers and boutiques. From traditional handicrafts to trendy goods, Orchid Magu provides a variety of shopping experiences.

Hulhumale Central Park: Located at Hulhumale, a reclaimed island in Male, Hulhumale Central Park is a popular gathering area for residents and tourists. It has a retail center with businesses providing apparel, accessories, and souvenirs.

Manta Plaza: Situated in the Hulhumale neighborhood, Manta Plaza is a contemporary retail complex that caters to varied preferences. It contains a range of retailers, including fashion boutiques, technology stores, and eating alternatives.

Champa Central Hotel: Champa Central Hotel, situated in Male, contains a shopping arcade with a variety of retail businesses.

Visitors may visit stores offering local crafts, apparel, and accessories.

Hulhumale Ferry Terminal: While largely a transit center, the Hulhumale Ferry Terminal also offers a commercial area. Visitors may discover stores offering apparel, gadgets, and refreshments, making it a great destination for some shopping therapy.

Dharubaaruge: Dharubaaruge, a famous conference facility in Male, also features a retail arcade. The center holds exhibits, trade fairs, and cultural events, offering visitors an opportunity to purchase traditional handicrafts, textiles, and souvenirs.

STO Trade Centre: Located in Male, the STO Trade Centre provides a variety of retail outlets, including apparel, cosmetics, and home products. It is a popular area for residents and visitors to purchase daily goods.

Mulee Aage: Mulee Aage, the official house of the President of the Maldives, offers a commercial center in the proximity. Visitors may visit stores offering traditional relics, local crafts, and souvenirs.

Velana International Airport: The primary international airport in the Maldives, Velana International Airport, provides a range of duty-free retail alternatives. Travelers may shop for premium goods, gadgets, cosmetics, and local souvenirs before their departure.

Majeedhee Magu Promenade: Located along the shore in Male, the Majeedhee Magu Promenade is a popular area for shopping and relaxation. Visitors may enjoy spectacular vistas while strolling through businesses providing apparel, jewelry, and handicrafts.

Whale Submarine Mall: Situated in Male, the Whale Submarine Mall is a remarkable retail complex constructed around an actual submarine. It features a choice of boutiques offering apparel, accessories, and souvenirs, giving a great shopping experience.

Island Bazaar: Located in Male, Island Bazaar is a well-known retail complex that provides a mix of local and international goods. Visitors may browse stores offering apparel, jewelry, and handicrafts, as well as enjoy a choice of food options.

Hulhule Island Hotel: Hulhule Island Hotel, situated near the airport, includes a retail arcade catering to guests' requirements. It provides duty-free shopping, upscale brands, and a range of local goods.

STO Maldives: STO Maldives is a prominent shopping center in Male that provides a broad selection of items. From electronics and home products to apparel and accessories, this mall delivers a one-stop shopping experience.

Le Cute: Situated in Male, Le Cute is a fashionable retail center that focuses on fashion and cosmetics. It includes a range of apparel shops, cosmetic boutiques, and accessories, making it a popular destination for fashion fans.

ADK Shopping Mall: ADK Shopping Mall, situated in Male, is a contemporary retail complex providing a variety of shopping alternatives. Visitors may discover apparel, gadgets, home products, and a food court for eating.

Seagull Cafe House: Seagull Cafe House, located in Male, is not simply a café but also offers a retail center. It provides a unique combination of coffee, cuisine, and retail therapy, with stores offering apparel, accessories, and local handicrafts.

Conclusion: While the Maldives is largely recognized for its natural beauty, the country's shopping malls give an exceptional retail experience. From premium brands to small shops, these 20 retail complexes provide a broad selection of shopping alternatives for both residents and visitors. Whether you're seeking fashionable goods, traditional handicrafts, or scrumptious food, the Maldives' shopping malls provide something for everyone, making them a shopper's dream in this tropical paradise.

BEST MUSEUMS IN MALDIVES

One option to dive further into the country's rich history is by touring its amazing museums. From ancient antiquities to contemporary art, these 20 top museums in Maldives give a compelling peek into the rich past of this lovely island.

National Museum, Male: Located in the capital city, Male, the National Museum is a must-visit for history buffs. Housed in the old Sultan's Palace, it shows a significant collection of items, including royal antiques, traditional costumes, ancient weapons, and historical documents.

Maldives Maritime Museum, Male: Dedicated to the country's nautical heritage, the Maldives Maritime Museum shows a variety of artifacts connected to fishing, boat-building, navigation, and maritime history. Visitors may examine replicas of traditional boats, learn about local fishing practices, and receive insights into the significance of the sea to the Maldivian way of life.

Maldives Islamic Centre, Male: The Maldives Islamic Centre is an architectural masterpiece that commemorates the nation's primary faith, Islam. This center comprises a mosque, a library, and a museum that shows religious treasures, including antique Qurans, calligraphy, and Islamic art.

Hukuru Miskiy Museum, Male: Situated inside the Hukuru Miskiy Mosque complex, this museum gives a look into the history and customs of Islam in the Maldives. Visitors may discover beautiful woodwork, old texts, and relics that show the country's unique combination of Islamic and Maldivian cultural traditions.

Maldives Natural History Museum, Male: Dedicated to the rich flora and wildlife of the Maldives, this museum delivers an immersive experience with exhibits that include preserved marine life, coral specimens, shells, and interactive displays on the country's environmental conservation initiatives.

Maldives Past Museum, Male: Located in a historic structure, the Maldives Heritage Museum emphasizes the country's cultural past via its collection of traditional costumes, household objects, musical instruments, and artworks. The museum presents a detailed overview of Maldivian customs and traditions.

Esjehi Art Gallery, Male: For art connoisseurs, the Esjehi Art Gallery is a must-visit. Showcasing the works of local artists, the gallery shows modern paintings, sculptures, and installations that provide unique views into the Maldivian art scene.

National Art Gallery, Male: This colorful gallery displays a broad collection of modern and traditional artworks from local and international artists. It presents recurring exhibits that cover many creative forms, includes paintings, photography, and multimedia projects.

Maldives National Museum of Art, Male: A refuge for art enthusiasts, this museum honors the vivid creative manifestations of the Maldivian people. Visitors may explore a broad selection of modern artworks, including paintings, sculptures, and installations, giving a glimpse into the country's growing art scene.

Maldives 3D Museum, Male: Combining art and technology, the Maldives 3D Museum provides a unique experience for tourists. Featuring immersive three-dimensional artworks, this museum invites visitors to become a part of the art itself, creating infinite picture possibilities and amazing moments.

Maldives Fish Market, Male: While not a typical museum, the busy Maldives Fish Market gives a realistic peek into the country's fishing sector. Visitors may watch the dynamic trade of freshly caught seafood, engage with fishermen, and learn about the significance of fishing to the Maldivian economy.

Baa Atoll UNESCO Biosphere Reserve Interpretation Centre, Baa Atoll: Located on Baa Atoll, a UNESCO Biosphere Reserve, this interpretive center teaches tourists about the value of biodiversity and conservation efforts in the Maldives. Through interactive displays, visitors may learn about the various marine life, coral reefs, and sustainable practices in the area.

Utheemu Ganduvaru, Haa Alif Atoll: Utheemu Ganduvaru is a historical landmark that gives a look into the life and times of Sultan Mohamed Thakurufaanu, a national hero. This museum shows objects, including traditional furniture, household items, and historical documents, offering insights into Maldivian history and the battle against colonialism.

Fuvahmulah Museum, Fuvahmulah Island: Situated on Fuvahmulah Island, this museum highlights the distinctive culture and history of the people. It shows antiques, pictures, and artworks that emphasize the island's peculiar customs, folklore, and natural marvels.

Maldives Victory Memorial Museum, Hulhule Island: Dedicated to the remembrance of the victims of the 1988 Maldives coup attempt, this museum gives a sobering reminder of the country's difficult history. Visitors may learn about the events surrounding the coup and offer their condolences at the monument.

Hithadhoo Regional Museum, Addu City: Located in Addu City, the Hithadhoo Regional Museum is a treasure mine of historical items. From local handicrafts to archaeological artifacts, this museum presents a thorough picture of the region's legacy, including the ancient Buddhist period and colonial influences.

Addu Atoll WWII Museum, Addu City: This museum examines the effects of World War II on Addu Atoll, which operated as a British Royal Air Force base throughout the war. Exhibits include wartime relics, pictures, and personal testimony, affording an insight into the island's participation in this worldwide battle.

Equator Village Museum, Gan Island: Situated at Gan Island, this museum is housed in a historic British RAF facility. It shows the island's colonial past and its transition into a vacation destination. Visitors may view images, souvenirs, and relics that reflect the island's history.

Thinadhoo Cultural Museum, Gaafu Dhaalu Atoll: The Thinadhoo Cultural Museum highlights the cultural legacy of the Gaafu Dhaalu Atoll. Exhibits include traditional clothing, tools, and relics that illustrate the distinct customs and traditions of the region's residents.

Naifaru Cultural Museum, Lhaviyani Atoll: This modest community museum on Naifaru Island gives a look into the native way of life. Visitors may learn about the island's fishing practices, view cultural relics, and connect with the friendly residents who are concerned about preserving their legacy.

Conclusion: Exploring the top museums in Maldives is an enlightening experience that enables tourists to dig into the country's unique history, lively culture, and natural beauty. From national museums in Male to provincial museums on the atolls, each museum gives a distinct viewpoint on the Maldivian past. Whether you are interested in ancient relics, modern art, or local customs, these museums give you a chance to engage with the rich fabric of Maldivian culture, making your vacation to this tropical paradise even more unforgettable.

BEST PARKS AND GARDENS IN MALDIVES

From lush foliage to vivid tropical flowers, these parks and gardens provide a calm getaway from the everyday grind. In this post, we will dig into the 20 greatest parks and gardens in the Maldives, offering extensive descriptions and emphasizing their distinct qualities.

Sultan Park (Rasrani Bageecha): Located in the capital city of Male, Sultan Park is a historical garden that previously belonged to the Sultan's Palace. Today, it provides a tranquil getaway with beautifully designed gardens, bright flowers, and shaded trees. The park also contains the National Museum, which is a must-visit for history buffs.

Islamic Centre Park (Hulhumale): Situated in Hulhumale, the Islamic Centre Park is a serene retreat with well-maintained grass and beautiful flower beds. It has amazing views of the Indian Ocean and contains a gorgeous mosque, making it a prominent religious and recreational location.

Villingili Botanical Garden (Addu City): Located in Addu City, Villingili Botanical Garden is a spacious sanctuary that highlights the rich biodiversity of the Maldives. The garden contains several plant varieties, including indigenous flora and medicinal herbs. Visitors may also enjoy walking paths and picnics in this serene location.

Malé City Park (Rasfannu): Malé City Park, commonly known as Rasfannu, is a popular recreational site in the capital. It has well-manicured lawns, vivid flower beds, and strolling trails. The park is a perfect area to relax, exercise, or have a picnic while taking in the spectacular views of the city skyline.

Hithadhoo Regional Park (Addu City): Hithadhoo Regional Park, situated in Addu City, is a wide green area that provides many facilities for guests. It features children's playgrounds, jogging tracks, and sports facilities. The park is great for outdoor activities and family trips.

Feydhoo Nature Park (Addu City): Feydhoo Nature Park, located in Addu City, is a natural reserve that highlights the distinctive flora and wildlife of the Maldives. The park is home to different bird species, unique vegetation, and mangroves. Visitors may explore the park's paths and enjoy birding possibilities.

Kudahuvadhoo Park (Dhaalu Atoll): Kudahuvadhoo Park, situated in Dhaalu Atoll, is a picturesque park with groomed grass and coconut palm trees. It provides a tranquil setting and an opportunity to enjoy the laid-back island lifestyle. The park is a wonderful area for a leisurely walk or a picnic.

Gan Regional Park (Laamu Atoll): Gan Regional Park, located in Laamu Atoll, is a lovely park recognized for its rich flora and picturesque splendor. It has a playground, picnic spots, and a running track. Visitors may relax in this tranquil area and appreciate the natural surroundings.

Veymandoo Recreational Park (Thaa Atoll): Veymandoo Recreational Park, situated in Thaa Atoll, is a well-maintained park that provides beautiful ocean views. It contains nicely designed gardens, seats, and a children's play area. The park is a fantastic area for relaxing and enjoying the sea wind.

Dharavandhoo Park (Baa Atoll): Dharavandhoo Park, located in Baa Atoll, is a tiny yet lovely park noted for its tropical flora and flowers. It offers a calm atmosphere for tourists to relax and appreciate the natural beauty of the surroundings.

Utheemu Ganduvaru Park (Haa Alif Atoll): Utheemu Ganduvaru Park, situated on Haa Alif Atoll, is a historical park linked with the house of Sultan Mohamed Thakurufaanu. The park has well-manicured grass, trees, and a playground. Visitors may explore the park's historical importance and relax in its serene ambiance.

Kurendhoo Park (Lhaviyani Atoll): Kurendhoo Park, located in Lhaviyani Atoll, is a delightful park with rich flora and a wonderful sandy beach. It provides a calm ambiance and is a great site for nature enthusiasts to immerse themselves in the island's tranquillity.

Kaashidhoo Regional Park (Kaafu Atoll): Kaashidhoo Regional Park, situated on Kaafu Atoll, is a picturesque park that provides a variety of leisure activities. It has jogging paths, a seashore, and picnic places. Visitors may enjoy swimming, sunbathing, or just taking in the amazing ocean views.

Dhidhoo Park (Haa Alif Atoll): Dhidhoo Park, located on Haa Alif Atoll, is a scenic park with a gorgeous lake in its center. It gives a calm ambiance and an opportunity to rest among nature's splendor. The park also provides opportunities for outdoor sports and recreation.

Maroshi Park (Shaviyani Atoll): Maroshi Park, situated on Shaviyani Atoll, is a well-maintained park with beautiful flower beds and shaded trees. It is a fantastic area for a leisurely stroll and enjoying the quiet of the island. The park regularly holds cultural events and festivals.

Kulhudhuffushi Central Park (Haa Dhaalu Atoll): Kulhudhuffushi Central Park, located in Haa Dhaalu Atoll, is a bustling park with finely planted gardens and a central fountain. It provides a peaceful ambiance and is a favorite meeting spot for residents and visitors alike.

Dhangethi Park (Alif Dhaalu Atoll): Dhangethi Park, situated in Alif Dhaalu Atoll, is a picturesque park that exhibits the natural beauty of the island. It has coconut palm trees, vivid flowers, and well-maintained walkways. The park offers a calm place for tourists to experience the island's sensations.

Maduvvari Park (Raa Atoll): Maduvvari Park, located on Raa Atoll, is a modest but lovely park with groomed grass and seats. It provides amazing views of the surrounding turquoise seas and is a favorite area for rest and contemplation.

Thinadhoo Park (Gaafu Dhaalu Atoll): Thinadhoo Park, situated in Gaafu Dhaalu Atoll, is a well-designed park with shade trees and strolling routes. It provides a tranquil place for tourists to relax and appreciate the beauty of the island. The park is also a popular place for cultural events and meetings.

Hulhudheli Park (Faafu Atoll): Hulhudheli Park, located in Faafu Atoll, is a picturesque park with well-manicured grass and colorful flowers. It gives a calm escape and a chance to admire the natural marvels of the Maldives.

Conclusion: The Maldives, famed for its magnificent beaches, also provide a variety of stunning parks and gardens that enable tourists to interact with nature. Whether you're seeking relaxation, a leisurely walk, or a location for outdoor sports, these 20 greatest parks and gardens in the Maldives give a calm getaway and a chance to fully enjoy this tropical paradise's natural splendor.

BEST NIGHT CLUBS AND BARS IN MALDIVES

The Maldives features a choice of top-notch nightclubs and bars that appeal to every taste. In this post, we will examine the 20 greatest nightclubs and bars in the Maldives, where you can dance the night away, sip inventive cocktails, and make amazing memories.

1 OAK Maldives: Located on the island of Finolhu, 1 OAK Maldives is a world-renowned nightclub that provides an elite nightlife experience. With top international DJs, beautiful furnishings, and an active environment, this club is a must-visit for party aficionados.

Subsix: Subsix, located six meters below the surface of the Indian Ocean in Niyama Private Islands, is a unique underwater nightclub. Offering breathtaking vistas of aquatic life and a sophisticated ambiance, Subsix gives a memorable party experience.

FEN Bar: Situated in the W Maldives resort, FEN Bar provides a stylish and dynamic environment. With a beachside setting, live DJ performances, and a broad range of beverages, FEN Bar is a popular option for travelers wanting a dynamic nightlife experience.

Baazaar: Located in the Fairmont Maldives Sirru Fen Fushi, Baazaar is a sophisticated and modern bar that mixes traditional Maldivian décor with contemporary features. The bar provides a comprehensive choice of unique drinks and live entertainment, making it a fantastic destination for a night out.

Longitude: Situated in the COMO Maalifushi resort, Longitude is a beachside bar with a laid-back and comfortable feel. Here, you may enjoy spectacular sunset views while sipping on unique drinks and listening to live music.

Beach Rouge: Found in the Lux South Ari Atoll resort, Beach Rouge is a popular beach club that provides a blend of Mediterranean and Maldivian tastes. With a chilled-out ambiance, poolside seats, and live DJ performances, Beach Rouge is excellent for anyone searching for a blend of leisure and enjoyment.

Club Med Kani: Club Med Kani delivers a dynamic and colorful nightlife experience. Situated on a secluded island, this all-inclusive resort provides themed events, live music, and a selection of entertainment options that appeal to all ages.

Vinum: Located in the Conrad Maldives Rangali Island, Vinum is a wine and cheese bar that offers a classy and private ambiance. With a large wine selection and a menu emphasizing gourmet cheeses, Vinum is great for those wanting a more sophisticated nightlife experience.

Deep End: Deep End, located in the Huvafen Fushi resort, is a sleek and modern bar with a spectacular beachside backdrop. Offering panoramic views, a laid-back environment, and live music, this pub is a perfect location to relax and enjoy the evening.

Lava Lounge: Found in the Outrigger Konotta Maldives Resort, Lava Lounge is a contemporary and fashionable bar that mixes traditional Maldivian architecture with modern architectural features. With its seaside setting, varied food, and live entertainment, Lava Lounge offers an entertaining night out.

Cocoon Beach Club: Located on Ookolhufinolhu Island, Cocoon Beach Club is a bustling beach club that provides a range of entertainment alternatives. From pool parties and themed evenings to live music performances and beachfront drinks, Cocoon Beach Club is popular among residents and visitors alike.

Mixe: Situated in the PER AQUUM Niyama resort, Mixe is a trendy and elegant seaside bar. With stunning views, comfy seats, and a wide beverage menu, Mixe creates an amazing ambiance for a night of leisure and socialization.

Glow Bar: Glow Bar, situated in the Crossroads Maldives, is a dynamic and active venue that provides a choice of entertainment alternatives. From live bands and DJ performances to themed events, Glow Bar offers an amazing night out.

Bubbles Bar: Located in the Hurawalhi Island Resort, Bubbles Bar is an underwater champagne bar, that provides a unique and wonderful atmosphere for an evening drink. Surrounded by the beautiful aquatic life of the Maldives, this bar provides a genuinely memorable experience.

Rah Bar: Situated in the Jumeirah Vittaveli resort, Rah Bar is a seaside bar recognized for its casual and laid-back environment. With spectacular ocean views, comfy seats, and a broad selection of drinks and nibbles, Rah Bar is the ideal area to relax and enjoy the Maldivian ambiance.

Sky Bar: Located in the Velassaru Maldives resort, Sky Bar is a rooftop location that provides panoramic views of the surrounding islands and ocean. With a trendy and modern décor, a broad range of beverages, and live music, Sky Bar is a great spot to view the sunset and enjoy a bustling nightlife.

Nika Bar: Found inside the Nika Island Resort & Spa, Nika Bar is a small and personal venue noted for its romantic environment. With candlelight tables, a broad drink menu, and occasional live music performances, Nika Bar is excellent for couples seeking a romantic night out.

Beach Club at LUX North Male Atoll: Situated in the LUX North Male Atoll resort, the Beach Club is a sleek and fashionable location with magnificent ocean views. Offering a selection of beverages, live entertainment, and a poolside location, the Beach Club is a fantastic alternative for anyone searching for a vibrant and sophisticated beach party.

Sip Bar: Located in the Baros Maldives resort, Sip Sip Bar is a modest and compact location that provides a calm and casual ambiance. With its beachside setting, tasty drinks, and friendly staff, Sip Sip Bar is great for a laid-back evening by the sea.

5.8 Undersea Restaurant and Bar: Situated five meters below the surface of the Indian Ocean at Hurawalhi Island Resort, the 5.8

Undersea Restaurant, and Bar provides a completely unique and amazing experience. With panoramic underwater views and a menu of inventive drinks, this bar offers an otherworldly environment for a night out.

Conclusion: The Maldives not only provides magnificent natural beauty but also a dynamic and thrilling nightlife scene. From world-renowned nightclubs to fashionable beach bars and unusual underwater locations, the Maldives offers something to satisfy every taste. Whether you're seeking a vibrant party environment or a peaceful seaside setting, these 20 top nightclubs and bars in the Maldives are guaranteed to give a memorable nightlife experience that compliments your tropical island holiday.

NIGHTLIFE IN MALDIVES

- **ROMANTIC EVENING**

It is an ideal place that provides couples a romantic sanctuary, suitable for making lasting memories. Among the different experiences, one may have in the Maldives; a romantic evening stands out as a genuinely spectacular occasion. This essay will look into the fascinating components that make a romantic evening in the Maldives a memorable experience.

Sunset Cruises: To commence your romantic evening, go on a sunset cruise over the peaceful seas of the Maldives. As the sun sets, painting the sky with vivid shades of orange and pink, you and your spouse may wallow in the spectacular beauty while enjoying each other's company. Sip on champagne, devour tasty canapés, and feel the soothing sea air as you float across the tranquil waters, creating a really romantic scene.

Seaside candlelight supper: Indulge in an intimate, seaside candlelight supper beneath the starlit sky. Picture a private length of immaculate beach, ornamented with gentle candlelight, and a table tastefully arranged for two.

As you luxuriate in exquisite food, carefully produced by famous chefs, you'll be serenaded by the sound of lapping waves. The small ambiance, along with the relaxing sounds of the ocean, produces an exceptional dining experience, making it a really beautiful night.

Overwater Villa Experience: The Maldives is famed for its exquisite overwater villas, and what better place to spend a romantic evening than in one of these private retreats? These magnificent rooms give direct access to the blue waves, enabling you to rest and unwind in utmost seclusion. Imagine basking in your own infinity pool, champagne in hand, while the sun slips beyond the horizon.

The breathtaking views of the infinite ocean from your villa create an aura of romance and tranquillity.

Couples Spa getaway: Pamper yourself with a couples' spa getaway, indulging in a world of relaxation and regeneration. Many resorts in the Maldives provide luxury spa treatments influenced by ancient healing procedures. Indulge in a romantic couple's massage, where experienced therapists will work their magic, taking away any stress and leaving you in a state of complete happiness. The calm environment, fragrant smells, and quiet music combine to provide an intimate and extremely relaxing experience.

Bioluminescent Beach: For an exceptional experience, check out the captivating bioluminescent beach in the Maldives. When the night falls, the ocean waters come alive with bioluminescent plankton, generating a bright blue light. Take a barefoot walk down the coast with your loved one, hand in hand, leaving sparkling footsteps behind. This natural phenomenon is nothing short of spectacular, delivering a unique and romantic interaction with nature.

Conclusion: A romantic evening in the Maldives is a genuinely wonderful experience. Whether you choose to sail into the sunset, savor a candlelit dinner on the beach, luxuriate in an overwater villa, indulge in a couple's spa retreat, or witness the enchantment of a bioluminescent beach, the Maldives offers an array of breathtaking experiences that cater to every romantic inclination. It is a resort that symbolizes romance, beauty, and calm, generating memories that will last a lifetime.

FESTIVALS AND EVENTS IN MALDIVES

Beyond its natural beauty, the Maldives is also a dynamic cultural destination, providing a broad assortment of festivals and events throughout the year. From religious observances to traditional festivals, these events give a unique glimpse into the rich traditions and customs of the Maldivian people.

This article tries to look into some of the most notable festivals and events that define the social and cultural fabric of the Maldives.

Eid-al-Fitr: Eid-al-Fitr, called locally as "Kuda Eid," is one of the most major Islamic celebrations in the Maldives. Celebrated at the completion of Ramadan, the Islamic holy month of fasting, Eid-al-Fitr represents a time of celebration and appreciation.

Locals assemble in mosques for prayers, share emotional greetings, and participate in acts of charity. Families gather together to enjoy feasts with typical Maldivian specialties, such as Radhika (short eats), masroshi (fish-filled pastry), and garudhiya (fish soup).

Independence Day: On the 26th of July, Maldivians remember their independence from British colonial authority, which happened in 1965.

This national holiday is celebrated with considerable excitement around the archipelago. The capital city of Malé becomes a hotbed of celebrations, with parades, cultural performances, traditional music, and bright demonstrations of national pride. It is a moment for Maldivians to reflect on their past and celebrate their sovereignty.

National Day: National Day, observed on the 1st of January, is an opportunity to honor the day the Maldives became a republic in 1953. Colorful parades, marching bands, and cultural events take place around the nation, displaying the variety and solidarity of the Maldivian people. The festivities also feature traditional sports activities, such as baibala (pole climbing), goma (a traditional game played with coconuts), and don hiyaa (a sort of wrestling).

Ramadan: Ramadan carries tremendous importance for Muslims worldwide, including in the Maldives. It is a month of fasting, prayer, and introspection. During this time, the streets of Malé and other inhabited islands come alive after nightfall, when families break their fast together.

The bustling mood is further heightened by the Ramadan bazaars, where residents and tourists may enjoy a variety of traditional foods, desserts, and cool beverages.

Cultural events: The Maldives also holds various cultural events that display the country's creative legacy. One such event is the Maldives Traditional Food and Cultural Festival, which highlights Maldivian food, music, dancing, and crafts. Visitors get the chance to enjoy genuine Maldivian delicacies, observe traditional performances, and mingle with local artists. The event gives a unique glimpse into the traditional way of living in the Maldives.

Whale Shark Festival: The Maldives is famed for its spectacular marine biodiversity, especially the majestic whale shark. The Whale Shark Festival, held on the southern atoll of Dhidhdhoo, commemorates the conservation efforts around these gentle giants. The event incorporates educational activities, environmental awareness campaigns, snorkeling and diving trips, and cultural performances. It provides a chance for tourists to learn about marine conservation while enjoying the natural beauty of the Maldives.

Conclusion: Festivals and events in the Maldives provide a dynamic and engaging cultural experience for both residents and tourists. These events highlight the customs, traditions, and religious activities that constitute the Maldivian way of life. From religious observances like Eid-al-Fitr and Ramadan to national festivals like Independence Day and National Day, these festivities give a look into the rich fabric of Maldivian culture. Whether it is relishing local food, experiencing enthralling performances, or participating in athletic activities, these festivals enable people to interact with the Maldivian community and make lasting memories in this tropical paradise.

HEALTH AND SAFETY IN MALDIVES

It's crucial to emphasize health and safety. By being well-prepared and knowledgeable, you can assure a pleasant and worry-free experience throughout your stay in this gorgeous area. This thorough travel guide will offer you vital information and practical advice to help you manage health and safety issues when visiting the Maldives.

Pre-Travel Considerations:

Travel Insurance: It is vital to have adequate travel insurance that covers medical emergencies, trip cancellations, and any other unexpected situations. Confirm that your insurance coverage includes medical evacuations, particularly if you intend to participate in risky activities.

Vaccinations and Health Check-ups: Consult your healthcare physician or a travel medicine expert at least 4-6 weeks before your trip to ensure you are up-to-date with regular immunizations. Additionally, enquire about particular immunizations advised for the Maldives, such as hepatitis A and B, typhoid, and influenza.

Drugs: If you use prescription drugs, ensure you have enough supply for the length of your vacation. Carry them in their original packaging, together with a copy of the prescription. It's also good to include a basic first aid kit with necessary materials like band-aids, antibacterial ointment, and pain medicines.

Water and Food Safety:

Drinking Water: It is suggested to consume bottled water or water that has been adequately treated and filtered. Most resorts and hotels supply clean drinking water, but if in doubt, consult with the staff.

Food Hygiene: The Maldives provides a rich dining experience, including fresh fish and indigenous delicacies. When eating at local restaurants, ensure the food is properly prepared and served hot. Opt for eateries with strong sanitary standards and great ratings.

Sun Safety:

Sunscreen & Protection: The Maldives boasts a tropical environment with plentiful sunlight. Protect yourself from damaging UV rays by using sunscreen with a high SPF, broad-brimmed hats, sunglasses, and lightweight clothing that protects your skin. Seek cover during high solar hours (10 am to 4 pm).

Hydration: Stay hydrated by consuming enough fluids, particularly while indulging in outdoor activities or spending a long time under the sun.

Marine Safety:

Snorkeling and Diving: The Maldives is famed for its gorgeous coral reefs, making snorkeling and diving popular pastimes. Prioritize your safety by picking licensed and recognized tour providers. Ensure that you obtain suitable equipment and listen to attention to the safety training. Respect aquatic life and use proper snorkeling and diving procedures.

Sea Conditions: Before setting out for water-based activities, verify the weather conditions and respect any warnings or advisories supplied by authorities or your hotel.

Mosquito-Borne Diseases: a. Dengue and Malaria: While the danger of these illnesses is quite low in the Maldives, it is recommended to take measures. Use insect repellents, wear long-sleeved clothes, and consider staying in hotels with screened windows or air conditioning.

COVID-19 Safety Measures: a. Travel Restrictions: Stay informed of the latest travel warnings and restrictions pertaining to COVID-19. Check the requirements for testing, quarantine, and immunization certifications before coming to the Maldives.

Hygiene and Social Distancing: Adhere to local health requirements, including wearing face masks, keeping physical distance, and exercising regular hand hygiene. Respect any unique procedures imposed by resorts, hotels, or tourist attractions.

Conclusion: By emphasizing health and safety factors, you may enjoy a delightful and worry-free holiday in the Maldives. Prepare in advance, be informed, and follow the recommendations offered by local authorities and your hotel. With its spectacular beauty and wonderful friendliness, the Maldives guarantees an amazing experience while maintaining your well-being during your stay.

PHARMACY AND FIRST AID

When going to the lovely tropical paradise of the Maldives, it is vital to have information about pharmacies and first aid services accessible on the islands. While the Maldives is famed for its stunning beaches and luxurious resorts, it's necessary to be prepared for any unanticipated conditions that may need medical treatment.

This travel guide contains thorough information about pharmacies, first aid facilities, and important things to bring to ensure a safe and worry-free journey to the Maldives.

Healthcare System in Maldives: The Maldives has a well-established healthcare system, principally focused in the capital city of Male. The Maldivian healthcare system encompasses governmental and private healthcare institutions. Public hospitals and health institutions are mostly concentrated in Male, although private clinics and pharmacies may be found on several inhabited islands and resort islands.

Pharmacies in the Maldives: Pharmacies, often known as "medical shops" or "drug stores," serve a critical role in delivering important pharmaceuticals and healthcare goods. In Male, the capital city, various pharmacies are accessible, frequently operating seven days a week. It's vital to know that pharmacies outside of Male can have restricted hours of operation. When touring the local islands or resort islands, it's important to pack any required prescriptions or medical supplies in advance.

Prescription Medications and Over-the-Counter Drugs:

If you need prescription prescriptions during your stay in the Maldives, it is advisable to pack enough supplies from your home country. It's usually recommended to bring the actual prescriptions or a statement from your doctor, outlining the contents of the drugs. Over-the-counter medications, such as pain relievers, antacids, and basic cold cures, are frequently accessible in pharmacies around the Maldives.

First Aid Services: In case of a medical emergency, the Maldives has well-equipped hospitals in Male, notably the Indira Gandhi Memorial Hospital. These hospitals offer emergency medical services and specialty treatments. Resort islands frequently include on-site medical clinics with qualified personnel that can give basic first aid and first medical care.

Essential First Aid Kit: It is advisable to bring a basic first aid kit while going to the Maldives. Some crucial elements to include are:

Adhesive bandages and sterile dressings for small cuts and wounds

Antiseptic solution or wipes for cleansing wounds

Pain relievers (such as paracetamol or ibuprofen)

Antihistamines for allergies or bug bites

Diarrhea relief medicine

Sunscreen with a high SPF and after-sun lotion

Insect repellant to prevent mosquito bites

Motion sickness medicine (if required)

Rehydration salts to counteract dehydration

Any personal prescription drugs you need

Conclusion: While the Maldives is surely a lovely place for a wonderful holiday, it's vital to be prepared for any unforeseen medical issues. Familiarize yourself with the locations of pharmacies, medical facilities, and first aid services accessible during your visit. By taking measures, packing a basic first aid kit, and ensuring you have appropriate drugs, you may enjoy a safe and worry-free holiday in the Maldives, knowing that you are prepared for any unforeseen medical circumstances.

CHAPTER 7

FOOD AND DRINK

• LOCAL DRINKS

The Maldives also features a rich and diversified food scene, featuring a vast choice of refreshing and delectable indigenous drinks. In this travel guide, we will examine 20 indigenous cocktails in the Maldives that you must taste during your stay. From traditional recipes to tropical pleasures, these drinks provide a fascinating glimpse of the Maldivian culture.

Kurumba: Let's start with the national drink of the Maldives - Kurumba. This delightful beverage is produced from the juice of young coconuts. It is generally served cold and is an excellent thirst quencher in the tropical environment.

Sai: Sai is a traditional Maldivian drink produced from toddy, a fermented sap collected from the bloom of the coconut palm. It has a somewhat acidic flavor and a low alcohol level, making it a favorite option among locals.

Raa: Similar to Sai, Raa is another alcoholic beverage created from fermented toddy. It is normally stronger than Sai and is commonly enjoyed by locals at festive events and social gatherings.

Mashuni Theluli: Mashuni Theluli is a wonderful beverage produced by combining fresh coconut water with grated coconut, milk, and a dash of cardamom. It is typically consumed as a morning drink or as a pleasant pick-me-up during the day.

Dhon Riha: Dhon Riha is a distinctive Maldivian drink created from the juice of the palmyra fruit. This sweet and tangy beverage is often drank during the Islamic month of Ramadan to break the fast.

Nannari Sharbat: Nannari Sharbat is a popular Indian-inspired drink found in the Maldives. It is produced from the extract of the Nannari root, combined with water, sugar, and a squeeze of lime. The outcome is a cold and refreshing drink that is great for hot days.

Kurumba Shake: Kurumba Shake is a wonderful combination of young coconut flesh, coconut water, and ice cream. It is a creamy and luscious drink that delivers a flavor of the tropics.

Raa Dhoru: Raa Dhoru is a unique beverage produced by combining Raa (fermented toddy) with lemon juice and sugar. This sweet and tangy cocktail is popular among residents and tourists alike.

Feli Dhun: Feli Dhun is a mixture of fresh passion fruit, lime juice, and sugar syrup. It is a spicy and lively drink that is great for individuals who appreciate tropical tastes.

Dhonkeyo: Dhonkeyo is a traditional Maldivian drink produced by infusing dried and crushed cucumber in water. It is a light and pleasant beverage that is great for keeping hydrated in a tropical environment.

Thambili Falhu: Thambili Falhu is a famous drink produced from the juice of the king coconut, a kind of coconut recognized for its sweeter flavor. It is an excellent thirst quencher and is generally served cold.

Black Tea with Ginger: While tea is not indigenous to the Maldives, it has become a mainstay in the local culture. Black tea with ginger is a popular option among locals and is commonly drunk with a splash of fresh lime.

Hot Spiced Coffee: For coffee enthusiasts, hot spiced coffee is a must-try in the Maldives. This fragrant beverage is produced by infusing freshly ground coffee with spices such as cinnamon, cardamom, and cloves.

Gulha Baiy: Gulha Baiy is a traditional Maldivian beverage produced by boiling water with ingredients including rice, sugar, and coconut. It has a thick and creamy consistency and is commonly served as a dessert.

Faluda: Faluda is a delicious dessert drink that originated in India but has become extensively liked in the Maldives. It is produced by blending milk, rose syrup, basil seeds, and vermicelli, creating a sweet and pleasant beverage.

Lime Juice with Mint: Simple but delicious, lime juice with mint is a popular cocktail enjoyed in the Maldives. Fresh lime juice is blended with sugar, water, and mint leaves to produce a cold and tart beverage.

Bandhi: Bandhi is a traditional Maldivian drink prepared with palm sugar, shredded coconut, and water. It is commonly drunk during traditional events and gives a distinct taste of native delicacies.

Nellika Vellum: Nellika Vellum is a health drink prepared from Indian gooseberry (Amla) juice combined with honey. It is thought to offer several health advantages and is widely ingested for its revitalizing powers.

Sambilla Tea: Sambilla tea is a herbal infusion prepared from the leaves of the sambilla plant. It has a mellow and calming taste and is commonly loved for its relaxing effects.

Iced Coffee with Coconut Milk: To fulfill your caffeine demands in a tropical style, try iced coffee with coconut milk. It blends freshly brewed coffee with cooled coconut milk, making it a creamy and rich beverage.

Conclusion: Exploring the indigenous beverages of the Maldives is a pleasant voyage into the country's culture and tastes. From ancient concoctions like Kurumba and Sai to refreshing tropical pleasures like Dhon Riha and Feli Dhun, these drinks provide a distinct and genuine experience for guests. Whether you're lazing by the beach or touring the bustling markets, don't miss the chance to enjoy these 20 native beverages in the Maldives and immerse yourself in the rich culinary traditions of this magnificent island paradise.

- **STREET FOODS**

Maldivian street cuisine provides a delectable assortment of tastes inspired by the country's rich culinary tradition. In this tour, we will take you on a gourmet adventure through the busy streets of Maldives, showcasing 20 must-try street dishes that will leave you hungry for more.

Hedhikaa: Hedhikaa, or Maldivian quick eats, are a mainstay of the local street food scene. These deep-fried or baked pastries are packed with diverse ingredients including fish, tuna, coconut, or veggies, providing a wonderful rush of flavors with every mouthful.

Masroshi: Masroshi is a typical Maldivian snack made from a thin bread foundation filled with a combination of fish, coconut, onions, and spices. It is then folded into a triangular form and either baked or fried until crispy.

Rihaakuru with Roshi: Rihaakuru is a rich and delicious fish paste, generally eaten with Roshi, a traditional Maldivian flatbread. The combination of these two street snacks gives a delightful taste that locals love.

Kulhi Boakibaa: Kulhi Boakibaa is a Maldivian fish cake prepared with minced fish, coconut, rice, and fragrant spices. It is cooked to perfection, resulting in a crispy outside and a juicy, savory inside.

Theluli Mas: Theluli Mas refers to grilled fish, a genuine seafood lover's pleasure. The fish is marinated in a combination of spices, coconut milk, and lime, then grilled over an open flame to accentuate its natural aromas.

Bis Keemiya: Bis Keemiya is a Maldivian spin on the ubiquitous samosa. It consists of a crispy pastry packed with a blend of minced fish or chicken, onions, and spices, producing a burst of delicious taste.

Mashuni and Roshi: Mashuni is a typical Maldivian meal prepared of shredded smoked tuna, coconut, onions, chili, and lemon juice. It is generally served with Roshi, producing a unique blend of textures and tastes.

Handulu Bondibai: Handulu Bondibai, also known as Maldivian doughnuts, are deep-fried balls of dough covered in sugar syrup. These delicious pastries are commonly consumed as a snack or dessert.

Kulhi Boakibaa Folhi: Kulhi Boakibaa Folhi is a version of the fish cake, where the minced fish mixture is wrapped in banana leaves and then grilled. The banana leaves infuse the fish with a subtle scent, improving its flavor.

Fihunu Mas: Fihunu Mas is a spicy grilled fish meal that captivates taste senses with its smokey flavor and scorching bite. The fish is marinated in a combination of chile, garlic, ginger, and other spices before being grilled to perfection.

Bis Keemiyaa Folhi: Bis Keemiyaa Folhi is a variant of Bis Keemiya where the tasty filling is wrapped in banana leaves and grilled. The banana leaves lend an earthy sent to the already tasty snack.

Bajiya: Bajiya is a famous Maldivian street snack, resembling a deep-fried dumpling. It is loaded with a variety of fish, onions, curry leaves, and spices, giving in a pleasant balance of textures and flavors.

Huni Roshi: Huni Roshi is a version of the classic Roshi bread, where grated coconut is blended with flour to make a distinctive dough. The bread is then baked on a griddle, imparting a slight coconut taste.

Theluli Mas Rihaakuru: Theluli Mas Rihaakuru mixes the taste of grilled fish with fish paste. The grilled fish is mashed and combined with Rihaakuru, producing a thick and flavorful dip that matches nicely with Roshi.

Gulha: Gulha is a delectable Maldivian delicacy prepared from a dough packed with a filling of fish, onion, chili, and shredded coconut. These bite-sized morsels are deep-fried to golden brown perfection.

Saagu Bondibai: Saagu Bondibai is a delicious dish created from sago pearls cooked in coconut milk and seasoned with cardamom and other spices. It is commonly eaten as a cooling dessert on hot days.

Dhon Riha: Dhon Riha is a famous street food dish prepared with grilled fish stewed in a spicy coconut curry. The fish absorbs the fragrant aromas of the curry, resulting in a wonderfully fulfilling supper.

Mashuni and Huni Roshi: Mashuni and Huni Roshi are a wonderful combination when Mashuni, the smoked tuna dish, is eaten with the classic Huni Roshi bread. The contrasting textures and tastes make it a pleasant snack.

Keemia Garudiya: Keemia Garudiya is a fragrant fish soup cooked with smoked tuna, onions, garlic, curry leaves, and spices. The soup is cooked to perfection, enabling the flavors to mix together harmoniously.

Maldivian Fudge: To conclude your street food experience on a sweet note, indulge in Maldivian fudge. Made with condensed milk, sugar, and different flavorings such as rose or cardamom, this melt-in-your-mouth dessert is a genuine joy.

Conclusion: Exploring the street food scene in Maldives is a chance to immerse you in the rich culinary culture of the nation. From spicy nibbles to sweet delights, the broad assortment of street meals provides a multitude of sensations that will leave you hungry for more. So, next time you visit the Maldives, be sure to step into the busy streets and sample these 20 street delicacies for a unique culinary experience.

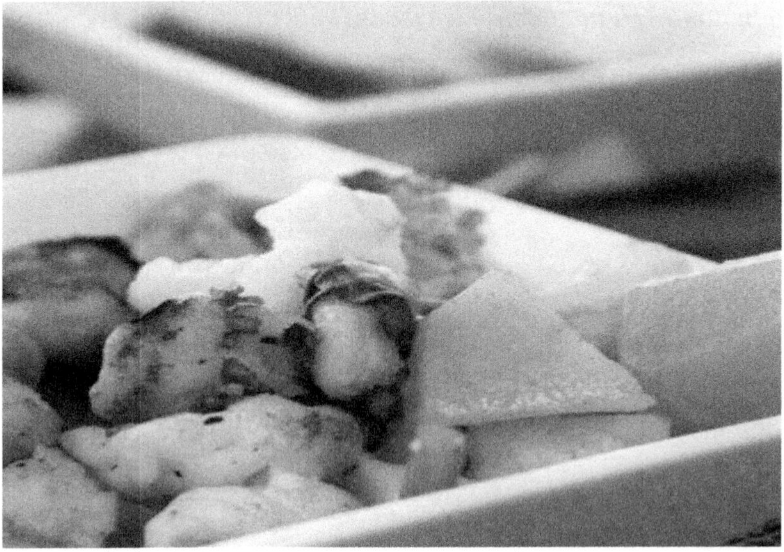

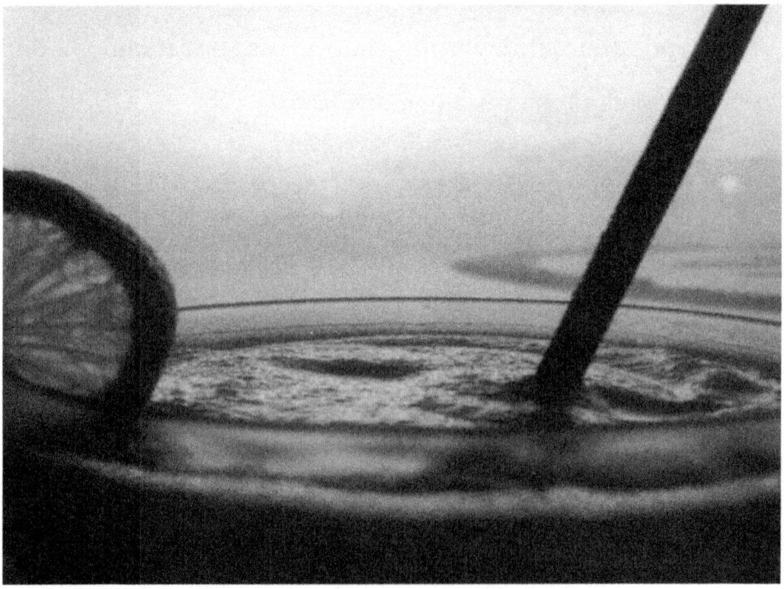

CONCLUSION

In conclusion, the Maldives travel guide for 2023-2024 demonstrates the ageless charm and enchantment of this tropical paradise. With its pure white sandy beaches, crystal-clear blue oceans and vivid coral reefs teaming with marine life, the Maldives continues to be a dream destination for tourists seeking ultimate relaxation, adventure, and natural beauty.

Travelers visiting the Maldives during this season may anticipate a flawless experience, as the nation has established precautions to safeguard the well-being and safety of tourists. From magnificent overwater villas to lovely beachside cottages, a broad choice of hotels caters to every traveler's interests and budgets.

The Maldives provides a wealth of activities for nature aficionados and adventure seekers alike. Snorkeling and diving lovers may explore the spectacular coral gardens and swim with stunning manta rays and whale sharks.

Water sports fans may participate in exhilarating activities such as kayaking, jet-skiing, and parasailing. Additionally, sunset cruises, island hopping, and fishing tours give a unique opportunity to immerse oneself in the local culture and experience stunning views.

For those seeking relaxation and renewal, the Maldives offers world-class spa facilities and wellness resorts. The tranquil ambiance of the islands paired with luxury spa treatments provides a delightful and refreshing experience.

Culinary connoisseurs will be thrilled by Maldivian cuisine, which mixes traditional tastes with foreign influences. From fresh seafood delicacies to savory curries and tropical fruits, the local gastronomy provides a pleasant gastronomic adventure.

It is crucial for tourists to be cognizant of the fragile ecology and to participate in sustainable tourism activities. The Maldives' dedication to environmental conservation is visible via several projects aimed at conserving the natural beauty and variety of the islands.